CONTENTS

This series of *Occasional Papers* was started in 1960 to supply the need for a medium of publication for studies in the field of social policy and administration which fell between the two extremes of the short article and the full-length book. It was thought that such a series would not only meet a need among research workers and writers concerned with contemporary social issues, but would also strengthen the links between students of the subject and administrators, social workers, committee members and others with responsibilities and interest in the social services.

Contributions to the series should be submitted to the Editorial Committee. A list of earlier papers in this series which are still in print is to be found on the back of this volume.

Richard M. Titmuss

SILENT IN COURT

The Legal Representation of Women
who Went to Prison

SUSANNE DELL

OCCASIONAL PAPERS ON SOCIAL ADMINISTRATION No. 42
*Editorial Committee under the
Chairmanship of Professor R. M. Titmuss*

*Published by G. Bell & Sons,
York House, Portugal Street, London, W.C.2*

MADE AND PRINTED IN ENGLAND BY
WILLMER BROTHERS LIMITED
BIRKENHEAD

ACKNOWLEDGEMENTS

The material on which this paper is based was collected in the course of a medico-social survey financed by the Home Office and conducted at Holloway prison. The project was carried out by the Institute of Psychiatry and the Institute for the Study and Treatment of Delinquency, under the direction of Professor T. C. N. Gibbens. The research workers were Mrs Joyce Prince, Miss Katharine Gillie, and myself.

The project would have been impossible without the friendly co-operation of both the staff and the prisoners in Holloway, to whom the warmest thanks are due. Valuable assistance was also given by probation officers and other agencies who supplied information. I am also very grateful to Mrs E. Maxwell for essential help in preparing the material.

The paper is published with the permission of the Home Office, to whom I am grateful for comments on an earlier draft. I alone am responsible for the views it contains.

December 1970   Susanne Dell

1. THE SURVEY

In 1967 a sample survey of the population of Holloway prison was undertaken, its object being to collect information about the social, medical and criminal background of the women sent there. Since Holloway receives about half of the country's female prisoners, it was hoped that the survey would give a representative picture of the women whom the courts imprison, whether on sentence remand.

The main purpose of the study was in no sense legal, but in th course of a pilot survey the interviewers were impressed by a numbe of features which made them feel it was important not to overlook th legal and administrative currents in the stream carrying women int prison. Among these was the fact that the majority of prisoner had no legal assistance, as a result of which they were often handicapped in important practical ways: for example, women were remanded in custody without understanding the procedures by which they could have asked for bail, or pleaded guilty to charges while ignorant of their legal implications. Very few of the unrepresented had felt able to speak up for themselves in the courtroom, and give the court any explanation of their behaviour. The most serious effect of this situation was that the women were therefore liable to be dealt with by courts that were unaware of important relevant or mitigating factors. This was especially true where social enquiry reports had not been called for.

In view of the practical importance to the prisoner of having legal assistance, information on this was recorded, and this report sets out the main facts and findings on the subject which came to light in the survey. Figures have not hitherto been available on the extent to which those in prison receive legal assistance.

The sample was selected between 1 January and 31 December 1967 from the daily prison reception lists. As it was the intake from Holloway's catchment area which was to be sampled, women who had been transferred from other prisons were excluded: every fourth of the other new[1] receptions was marked for interview. All cases were included, those remanded before trial, or after conviction, as well as fine defaulters, civil prisoners and those sentenced to imprisonment or Borstal training; the survey thus covered a quarter of the prison's annual intake, excluding transfers from other prisons or remand centres. The sample consisted of 638 women who between them accounted for 711 new receptions; a third of them mainly remands for psychiatric reports) were under the age of 21. Since Holloway receives about half of the country's female prisoners — the catchment area covers the courts south east of a line between the Wash and Lyme Bay — the sample represented about an eighth of all the women received into prison in 1967 in England and Wales.

The women were interviewed by one of three female research workers, and 250 of them were also seen by the psychiatrist directing the project. It was stressed that interviews were voluntary and confidential, and that the undertaking was independent of the prison authorities. The interviews were not structured, and usually lasted between one and two hours. The women were asked about their life histories, family environment, health, and their present situation, including the current charges against them: questions about the court proceedings and legal aid accounted for only a minor part of the interview.

Of the 638 women, 565 (89 per cent) were interviewed. Most of those who were not seen were released before interviews could be arranged, either because the remand period was short, or because they paid their fines or debts promptly, or because they were bailed. Five women were too ill to be seen, and in two cases there were insuperable language difficulties. Seven women declined to be interviewed.

After the women had been seen, corroborative information was sought from all available sources. The prison records showed whether they had applied for legal assistance, whether they had received replies to their applications, and whether they had been visited by a solicitor or solicitor's clerk. Prison hospital records contained social and psychiatric histories, and probation officers provided full reports on many of the women and were generally able to say whether they had been legally represented. Information from other agencies, such as mental hospitals, was also obtained. Particulars about previous convictions were furnished by the Criminal Record Office and details of recent mental hospital admissions were provided by the Department of Health and Social Security. Thanks to the help of all these agencies, corroborative information of various kinds was available for most of the sample, and this report is based on the combined information received from all the available sources, including the interview. There were of course some areas where it was not possible to check the women's accounts and where relevant, attention is drawn to these in the following pages.

NOTES

1. By ensuring the sample was drawn only from new receptions, the re-selection of women who were received into prison more than once on the same charge was avoided.

2. LEGAL REPRESENTATION: THE FACTS

In an adversary system of law the absence of legal help is inevitably a major handicap to a person on a criminal charge: a lawyer can advise on the plea, help to formulate and conduct the defence, and bring to the court's knowledge any relevant mitigating circumstances. Lack of legal assistance will put the accused at a disadvantage whatever the nature of the case, but the handicap is most serious where the liberty of the defendant is at stake and the outcome of the court appearance may be a period in prison, on remand or otherwise: in that situation lawyers may certainly be regarded as 'necessities not luxuries'.[1]

Table 1 on page 11 shows the extent to which the women were represented on the first occasion they came into the sample: 15 prisoners who were not charged with criminal offences are excluded from the table and the report. It should be noted that the study predates the introduction of the contributory legal aid system in 1968; how far this and other changes since 1967 may have affected the situation disclosed by the survey is discussed in Section 9.

Table 1 shows a very marked difference between the courts. Of the magistrates' court cases, only 17 per cent were known to be represented,[2] while in the higher courts the rate was 74 per cent. Of the 84 women sentenced to imprisonment by the magistrates' courts, only 14 (17 per cent) were represented: in the higher courts, of 68 sentenced to imprisonment or Borstal training 55 (81 per cent) were represented. Thus, it is the situation in the magistrates' courts that is the most disturbing, and it was these courts which dealt with 80 per cent of the prisoners.

In 1964 a Departmental Committee was appointed under the chairmanship of Mr Justice Widgery, to examine the arrangements for providing legal aid in criminal proceedings. The Committee examined the question of when the interests of justice required a defendant to be legally represented, and in its report of 1966[3] it detailed the circumstances in which it believed representation to be necessary. The first of these was a case where 'the charge is a grave

TABLE 1

Legal Representation in Magistrates' and Higher Courts

| Reason in Prison | Sentencing Courts | | | |
| | Magistrates' Courts | | Higher Courts | |
	No.	%	No.	%
Sentence of Imprisonment or Borstal Training (whether or not previously remanded)				
Represented	14	17	55	81
Unrepresented	68	81	13	19
Not known whether represented	2	2	—	—
Total	84	100	68	100
Remanded untried and not subsequently imprisoned				
Represented	44	35	36	73
Unrepresented	49	38	—	—
Not known whether represented	35	27	13	27
Total	128	100	49	100
Remanded after conviction and not subsequently imprisoned				
Represented	24	12	11	50
Unrepresented	161	79	7	32
Not known whether represented	19	9	4	18
Total	204	100	22	100
Imprisoned in lieu of fine				
Represented	—	—		
Unrepresented	57	84		
Not known whether represented	11	16		
Total	68	100		
Total—all women				
Represented	82	17	102	74
Unrepresented	335	69	20	14
Not known whether represented	67	14	17	12
Total	484	100	139	100

Definitions:

In this table, and throughout this paper, 'Magistrates' Court Cases' mean those in which the accused was sentenced or acquitted in the lower courts. 'Higher Court Cases' means those sent to Quarter Sessions or Assize Courts for trial or sentence. 'Represented' means that the defendant was represented, or had other legal help, at the sentencing (or acquitting) court. The description of a remanded person as 'represented' does not mean that she had legal help before or during her stay in prison; she may only have had it after her release. The stage at which the women who were represented first had contact with their lawyers is discussed in Section 6(2).

The term 'untried remand' means that the woman was remanded in custody before her trial. 'Convicted remand' means that she came into custody after being found guilty, but before being sentenced: the magistrates' court cases were remanded for medical and social reports under Sections 14 or 26[4] of the Magistrates' Courts Act 1952; most of the high court cases were women committed for sentence.

Some women, having been remanded once, would be returned to prison on a different type of remand. For example, persons first remanded before trial might, after conviction, be remanded for medical reports: in the table women are shown under the court which eventually sentenced them, but under the type of remand on which they first came into custody. The exception to this is women sentenced to imprisonment or Borstal training, who are all shown together in the table, irrespective of any preceding remands.

11

one, in the sense that the accused is in real jeopardy of losing his liberty' (paragraph 180). The Committee, when they talked of 'losing liberty' may only have had custodial sentences in mind, but those who are remanded in custody, or imprisoned in default of fine payments are deprived of their liberty as effectively, and often with equally serious repercussions, as those who serve sentences: they suffer the same loss of reputation, and not infrequently, lose jobs and accommodation as a consequence of their imprisonment. Tables 2, 3 and 4 on pp. 13, 14 and 15 show the extent to which, by each of these methods, women lost their liberty without being represented.

As one might expect, Table 2 shows that the proportion of unrepresented women decreases as the length of sentence increases, but there remained a significant group who were sentenced to substantial periods in prison, and who had no legal help. In particular, the proportion of girls sentenced to Borstal training without being represented—almost a third—was disturbing. This is a sentence which inevitably has a profound and permanent effect on an adolescent's development, and a young girl facing it unrepresented, with no-one to press the arguments against it, must be seriously handicapped.

How long the sixty-eight women who were imprisoned in default of payment of fines actually spent in prison is shown in Table 3 on page 14. Fifty-seven of these women were known to have had no legal help, but for eleven who paid their fines before they could be interviewed, information was not available. Only sixteen of the fine defaulters had been allowed time to pay their fines.

Although Table 3 shows that the sentences on fine defaulters were sometimes quite short, a number of women—mainly chronic alcoholics—in fact spent long periods in prison, coming in again and again in default of fines which they were unable to pay, serving, as they put it, 'life sentences on the instalment plan'. When their records for 1967 were examined it was found that some of these women had served the equivalent of substantial prison sentences without ever having legal assistance : for example, two alcoholics spent nine months of the year inside Holloway in default of fine payments: as remission does not apply to fine defaulters this meant that they served the equivalent of twelve month sentences. Several other women spent between four and eight months of the year in prison through failure to pay fines.

Since those who are imprisoned in default of fines are in prison not for their offences but for their failure to pay, their incomes were of some interest. The information collected was not at all complete, but it was found that at least twenty of the fifty-two women who were refused time to pay had either no income, or were on national assistance[4]. The poverty of those imprisoned for drunkenness was

12

TABLE 2

Custodial Sentences: Legal Representation and Length of Sentence

Length of sentence	Unrepresented		Represented		Representation not known	Total		
	Magistrates' Courts	Higher Courts	Magistrates' Courts	Higher Courts	Magistrates' Courts	Sentenced No.	Unrepresented No.	%
Under 3 months	45	—	5	1	2	53	45	85
3 months to 6 months	16	1	6	9		32	17	53
Over 6 months–1 year	4	3	3	14		24	7	29
Over 1 year	—	3	—	18		21	3	14
Borstal training	—	6	—	13		19	6	32
Borstal recall*	3	—	—	—		3	3	100
Total	68	13	14	55	2	152	81	53

*after a fresh conviction.

Table 3

Women Imprisoned in Default of Payment of Fine (none known to be represented)
Length of Sentence Imposed and Served

Sentence Imposed in Lieu of Fine	Total		Released on admission or within 5 days		Served 6 days but less than ¾ of sentence		Served ¾ of sentence or more	
	No.	%	No.	%	No.	%	No.	%
14 days or less	23		8		1		14	
15 days–1 month	29		6		8		15	
Over 1–3 months	16		10		2		4	
Total	68	100	24	35	11	16	33	49

TABLE 4

Remanded Women Not Subsequently Imprisoned
Legal Representation and Period in Prison

| | Total | | Time Spent in Prison | | | | | | | | |
| | | | 1–15 days | | 16–22 days | | 23–26 days | | 27–57 days | | 58 + days |
	No.	%	No.	%	No.	%	No.	%	No.	%	No.
Magistrates' Courts											
Represented	68	100	40	59	14	20	9	13	4	6	1
Not Represented	210	100	128	61	58	27	18	9	6	3	—
Not known whether represented	54	100	40	74	10	18	3	6	1	2	—
Total	332	100	208	63	82	25	30	9	11	3	1
Higher Courts											
Represented	47		10		9		7		12		9
Not represented	7		2		1		2		1		1
Not known whether represented	17		14		—		1		2		—
Total	71		26		10		10		15		10

particularly marked and it was unrealistic to suppose that the chronic alcoholics could often have avoided imprisonment by paying their fines.[5] Of the thirty-three women who served their terms fully or nearly fully, the incomes of ten were not known, but seventeen, i.e. over half, were known to be without incomes or on national assistance.

Almost two thirds of the sample were remanded in custody and not subsequently given custodial sentences; whatever the legal fiction, these women in effect served short sentences of imprisonment and Table 4 on page 15 shows their legal representation, and how long they spent in prison. It will be seen that eleven women were in custody for more than eight weeks; seven of these spent between nine and ten weeks there respectively for thirteen, seventeen, twenty-three and twenty-four weeks.

NOTES

1. Justice Hugo L. Black, in the American Supreme Court, 1963; Gideon v Wainwright.
2. For the sense in which this word is used throughout the paper, see the definitions below Table I
3. Report of the Departmental Committee on Legal Aid in Criminal Proceedings Cmnd. 2934. H.M.S.O.
4. Although Section 26 omits the word 'conviction', the court having only to be 'satisfied that the offence has been committed by the accused', cases remanded under S.26 are throughout this report included in the figures for 'convicted remands' since there was no practical distinction in the way the courts used Sections 14 and 26 for the purpose of obtaining post-trial medical reports.
5. As it was then called: now Supplementary Benefit.
6. Section 31 of the Magistrates' Courts Act 1952 requires courts in fixing the amount of a fine to 'take into consideration among other things, the means of the person', but it is common practice for the courts to fine destitute persons, e.g. for drunkenness and then to imprison them for failure to pay. The Criminal Justice Act 1967 has not restricted this practice and only requires the court to satisfy itself, before imprisoning, that there is no way of extracting payment. The Advisory Council on the Penal System in its report 'Non Custodial and Semi Custodial Penalties' (1970 H.M.S.O.) discussed the unsatisfactory nature of this situation, and held that fined offenders 'should not be committed to prison if they have failed to pay . . . solely for want of the means to do so' (para. 26). Methods of ensuring this are discussed in paras. 27–8 of the report.

3. LEGAL REPRESENTATION : THE NEED

Many of the women who were unrepresented were seriously handicapped by the lack of legal help. An inexperienced defendant is at a disadvantage in court even if well educated and articulate,[1] but for those who have little education, who are scared, nervous and unable to express themselves in the kind of language they believe is expected in court, the handicap can be crippling, particularly if they wish to deny the offence or to plead mitigating circumstances. Most of the unrepresented women suffered these handicaps to some degree, and their situation is discussed in sub-section (1) below. The following sub-sections (2-6) draw attention to the problems of five groups among whom lack of legal assistance involved particular hardship.

(1) *Handicaps of the unrepresented*

The problems of the unrepresented may begin before they reach the court room, and this subject is discussed in Section 4. But when the unrepresented defendant first appears in court, she is in several ways at a disadvantage. The proceedings may be bewildering and unintelligible to her to an extent which the court can hardly appreciate. One remanded girl, when asked by the interviewer whether she had asked for bail in court, replied 'What is bail? Is it the same as legal aid?'. Many others, even by the time they were interviewed, were confused about the correct meaning of terms like 'remand' and 'bail'. This kind of ignorance was not restricted to first offenders, although for them the position is particularly difficult; they do not know what to expect, how to behave, when to speak, and when to be silent. As one girl put it, 'I kept being told to get up and sit down'. It is not easy in such circumstances to do justice to one's own defence.

Frequently, the women said that they had not been able to catch what was being said: a typical comment was 'The judge mumbles away, and you don't know whether or not he's supposed to be speaking to you.' Many remanded women said they had left the court room without realizing what the magistrate had decided:

17

and it was then the police who had had to explain to them that they could not go home, as they had been remanded to Holloway. One first offender who caught the words 'two weeks' thought she was being put on probation for that period, until the police informed her in the cells that she was being remanded to prison for a fortnight. This ignorance and lack of understanding is a practical handicap to the unrepresented. If a woman who has been remanded in custody is not aware of the fact before she leaves the court room, she cannot ask for bail. Nor can she ask for it if she does not understand the meaning of the term. If she is remanded in custody for medical reports while unaware—as virtually all such women were—that bail could be granted for such a purpose, ignorance again precludes her from asking for it.[2] When a person is represented, her ignorance on such matters is immaterial : her solicitor will ask for bail, and present what arguments there may be against the use of custody. But it is unrealistic to assume that most unrepresented persons can properly look after their own interests in these matters; an illustration of this is given below, where a young girl who had been unrepresented when remanded in custody, was released when her father brought in a solicitor to argue the case for bail.

Case 549
A seventeen year old girl, with no previous convictions, was an in-patient in a mental hospital. When out for the day, she stole a dress from a local shop and was arrested. She appeared in court, unrepresented; pleaded guilty and was at once remanded to Holloway for three weeks for psychiatric reports.

She was fortunate in having a father who was concerned about her. He engaged a solicitor, who persuaded the court that the reports could as effectively be made from the hospital, and she was granted bail to return there. She was released after four days in prison. Had she had legal help at the outset she would never have come to Holloway: without it, she would have spent the full three weeks there.

The impossibility of expressing themselves in court weighed heavily on many women: not infrequently those who had given the interviewer full accounts of the background to their offences, said that the court had not known of the mitigating circumstances, as they had found themselves tongue-tied and silent at the appropriate moment. Several remanded women who were unrepresented asked the interviewers to come to court and 'speak for' them. Although the Widgery Committee thought that legal aid should rarely be necessary for the purpose of putting forward mitigating circumstances, there was evidence in the present study that the lack of it often meant that the courts were left unaware of im-
18

portant relevant matters. This was most often the case when social enquiry reports had not been asked for.[3] A few women complained that they never had a chance to explain themselves in court (this probably reflected their failure to understand the procedure) but the most common situation among the unrepresented was that when invited to do so, they failed to give the court any explanation of their behaviour. When asked 'What have you to say?' they seemed to think that the response expected was a short stereotype like 'I'm sorry' and they felt it impossible and inappropriate in the formality of the atmosphere to talk about the background to their offence. One woman described her feelings when she was invited to speak in court and failed to respond, much as she wished to : 'I was too overawed and frightened ... I didn't want to make a fool of myself ... I would only have cried.'

The following example gives some indication of the way in which an offender is handicapped by lack of legal assistance in putting forward pleas in mitigation.

Case 293

A woman of twenty-seven with three children aged between one and nine years, was accused on two charges of receiving. She had no previous convictions. She was married to a feckless husband, and at the time of the offence was in severe financial difficulties. She made a full statement to the police on arrest; was bailed overnight, and the next day went to court, having had no legal advice. She pleaded guilty, said nothing on her own behalf, and was sentenced to six months imprisonment. Social enquiry reports were not asked for.

A feature in this case was the woman's confidence that the police to whom she had related all the mitigating circumstances, would present these to the court. Unaware that this is no part of the police function, she was then surprised to find that only a very brief account of the offences was given to the court, and that the background to the case never emerged.

Once in Holloway this woman got legal aid for an appeal, and was subsequently put on probation, though not until she had served a considerable part of her sentence.

The lack of a lawyer to protect her interests can be an important handicap to the accused even where special mitigating circumstances are not involved. There were, for example, a few cases in which women were remanded or imprisoned in circumstances which seemed to involve general principles of civil liberty; yet because these prisoners were unrepresented, the issues could not be raised. The cases concerned women who had been remanded in custody, and for whom, on medical grounds, longer periods in custody were recommended by the prison doctors. In two instances women who had been remanded for three weeks for social and medical reports were found in prison to be suffering from venereal disease. One was an eighteen year old girl on probation for a drugs offence who was remanded because she failed to report to her probation officer; the other was a woman of twenty-four who was remanded after being found guilty of possessing an offensive weapon. Although the usual way of dealing with girls who needed V.D. treatment after a period in custody was to arrange for them to attend outside clinics, in these cases the medical reports to the magistrates suggested that further remands in custody should be imposed, so that treatment could be completed. In both cases the courts accepted the advice. No other medical or psychiatric recommendations were made. A third case involved an eighteen year old girl, accused of soliciting, who pleaded not guilty, and was remanded in custody before trial; medical reports were not requested. On routine examination, she was found to be suffering from venereal disease and a report was sent to the court stating that the girl was a known source of infection, and a clinic defaulter, and asking for her to be remanded again to allow time for the infection to be cleared up. When the girl returned to court, she was found guilty, and remanded in custody for two further weeks for 'medical enquiries' at the end of which she was fined £5.

The last of these cases was of a rather different nature and concerned a woman aged thirty-six suffering from paranoid schizophrenia. She came to Holloway for medical reports, having been arrested for soliciting. A report was made saying that she was unlikely to respond to psychiatric treatment and suggesting that a probation order would have therapeutic and supportive value. However, while in prison it was found that she was in need of a cervical cancer operation, which she refused to have. A further medical report was then presented by the prison advising 'that it would be better to sentence her in her own interests' so that she could be persuaded to have the operation. A two months sentence was imposed but she still refused the operation.

Cases of the above kind were rare—among 460 remanded women, four came to the interviewers' notice. Nevertheless, they raised important issues. Although the courts and doctors were acting in what they believed to be the best interests of the women's health, it is a questionable practice to use sentences or remands in custody for the purpose of ensuring that accused persons receive physical medical treatment which, if they were at liberty, they might refuse. When such persons are unrepresented, they have no protection in a situation of this kind.

20

(2) *The mentally handicapped*

The Widgery Committee held (paragraph 177) that in the interests of justice, there should be legal representation when an accused person was suffering from mental disorder or was incapable, through mental disability from conducting his own defence. How far was this the case among the sample?

The women were classified as to their current or recent mental health. The psychiatrist directing the enquiry interviewed 250 of them, and for many others, reports from the prison medical officers and psychologists and from outside hospitals were available.

Among those sentenced to imprisonment, just under half (sixty-nine) were found to be suffering from some form of mental disorder; 40 per cent of these were diagnosed as personality or behaviour disorders, 23 per cent were addicted to alcohol or drugs, and the remainder were cases of subnormality, neurosis, psychosis, etc. There was no significant difference in the rate of representation among those who were mentally ill and well. In the lower courts, nearly 90 per cent (thirty-four) of the thirty-nine imprisoned women with mental disorder were unrepresented: in the higher courts, the proportion was 17 per cent (five) of thirty disordered women. In some of the milder cases of mental ill-health, such as personality disorders, the lack of legal help may have been no greater hardship than it was to other women. But those who were subnormal or psychotic (five such unrepresented women were imprisoned by magistrates' courts) were incapable of conducting their own cases properly and some of those whose offences were connected with their mental illness were severely handicapped by the lack of a lawyer to assemble and present the full psychiatric evidence on their behalf. An example is outlined below:

Case 294

A married woman of thirty-nine, living with her husband and three children, aged between nine and thirteen. She had a long history of neurosis with compulsive shoplifting and had had both in- and out-patient treatment for years. She was a respectable, conscientious person who was ashamed and disturbed at her inability to control the urge to shoplift. She always stole articles of small value, usually groceries, which she was anxious to return afterwards. She was on probation and had an excellent relationship with her probation officer.

She committed a further offence and was sent to Quarter Sessions for sentence. A probation report was submitted which made no direct recommendation and a medical report from Holloway was also asked for. This was very short—described her as physically fit and made no recommendations beyond saying that 'No further psychiatric treatment at the present stage of her chronic psycho-neurosis is likely to be of help in overcoming her compulsive shoplifting'.

The Court did not suggest that this woman should apply for legal aid, and it did not occur to her to ask for it. She said nothing at the hearing and was sentenced to twenty-one months imprisonment.

Of the sixty-eight women imprisoned by magistrates in default of fines forty-one (60 per cent) were suffering from some form of mental disorder and all of them were known to be unrepresented. Alcoholism was the most common illness, affecting twenty-eight of the women; another four were psychotic, and two were subnormal.

Among the 403 women who were remanded in custody and not subsequently imprisoned 214 had some kind of mental disorder. Twenty-seven of these were sentenced by the higher courts, three being unrepresented; 187 were sentenced by magistrates, and 66 per cent of them (123) were unrepresented, including seventeen psychotic and fourteen subnormal women. In both courts the representation rate of those who were mentally disordered was similar to that of the women with normal mental health.

Apart from their recommendation that legal aid should normally be granted to the mentally disabled, the Widgery Committee had also advised that it should be given to those who were in danger of being compulsorily confined to a mental institution. Theoretically, this might have been the outcome for any of the 230 women for whom pre-sentence medical reports were requested: over 70 per cent of these (165) were unrepresented. In the event, only fifteen of the 230 women were compulsorily sent to hospital under Section 60 of the Mental Health Act 1959. Three were sent by the higher courts, and all were represented: twelve were sent by the lower courts, eleven were unrepresented, and for one there was no information.

Thus, as far as prisoners from the lower courts were concerned, the survey showed that the Widgery recommendations about granting legal aid to mentally disordered defendants were far from being fulfilled. Of fifty-four women who were psychotic or subnormal, 78 per cent (forty-two) were unrepresented, and among all 267 women with some kind of mental disability, three-quarters (198) were not represented. Probably the main reason for this is that magistrates have no way of recognizing the mentally handicapped when they appear in court : expert pre-trial interviewing of all defendants would be needed, if those who lack the mental ability to follow the proceedings are to be identified. The Widgery Committee did not discuss this difficulty.

In the higher courts the situation of the mentally handicapped was more satisfactory; no psychotic or subnormal prisoners were unrepresented, and of fifty-seven women with mental disorders, the proportion unrepresented was 14 per cent (eight).

(3) Prisoners from abroad

The Widgery Committee held that in the interests of justice, legal representation was necessary for 'persons whose knowledge of English was insufficient to enable them to understand the charge, or follow the proceedings properly' (paragraph 177). How many such people were found among the sample, and to what extent were they legally represented?

Ten per cent of the sample—sixty-two women—had been born outside the U.K. and Ireland, but only the twenty-four women from European countries were affected by language problems; all the other non-English women came from English-speaking areas (U.S., Canada, Jamaica, etc.). Two of the Europeans were released before interviews could be arranged. Of the women who were seen, ten were found to have no English at all, or a very poor knowledge of it: six of these had no legal assistance. The English of the other twelve was assessed as fair or good: and seven of them were unrepresented.

The difficulties of some of these foreign women arose not only from their language problems, but also from their social isolation; many had only been in the country a few months. This meant that at the time of arrest, court appearance, or dispatch to Holloway, they had no-one to turn to for help or advice. Legal help would at least have ensured that their position was fully explained to them, that bail applications were made when necessary, and that the courts were given full information. The problems of some of these women may be illustrated by the following example. Had this girl had her family to turn to, she would never have committed such an offence; and had a spokesman been able to explain her situation to the court it is unlikely that she would have been remanded to prison.

Case 036

An eighteen year old French girl of good character; she had left school six months earlier, and came to England au pair to learn the language. Her knowledge of English was still poor.

After her first job she went to stay with a girl friend, while seeking a new post which would allow her sufficient time to attend classes. She had some money to tide her over, but this was stolen from her. She felt she could not stay on with her friend without paying her share, and left. She had no-one to turn to. Someone told her she could sleep for the night in a derelict building, and she did so. With several others she was arrested there early the next morning and charged with 'wandering abroad'. She was taken to court, had no contact with any legal adviser, and was remanded to Holloway for medical and social enquiries. On her return to court the reports stated that she was an ordinary, non-deviant girl, in need of temporary accommodation, and she was discharged.

(4) *First offenders*

For a woman who is well entrenched in a criminal career, a three months sentence spent among her friends and in familiar surroundings may be, at worst, a hazard of her trade and at best a welcome break. But for the first offender even a three week remand in the prison hospital for medical reports will be a searing experience. If she is from a conventional background and without criminal contacts, for example a housewife convicted of shoplifting, the encounter with her fellow-prisoners may be the most frightening element. She will meet people of whose existence she had never known—drug addicts, prostitutes and lesbians, whose behaviour and attitudes may sicken her; and the uncontrolled behaviour of the more disturbed women, particularly the cell banging at night, will be a source of fear and alarm. While she has to face this she is cut off from all normal contacts with family and friends, deprived of her possessions and locked alone into a cell for hours on end. In addition to these difficulties is the feeling of shame and degradation of being in prison and being known to be there, of writing home on headed prison paper and (in 1967) of wearing prison clothes.

The Widgery Committee, in considering when the interests of justice required a defendant to be legally represented, regarded a real risk of disgrace, or serious damage to reputation, as a qualifying circumstance (paragraph 171). As an example they cited the case of a respectable housewife charged with shoplifting, where, they believed, the shame of conviction was likely to outweigh any penalty inflicted. This shame is many times multiplied when the 'respectable' defendant is sent to prison, whether on sentence or remand.

One-third of the sample (206 women) had no previous convictions.[4] The following table shows the proportion who were represented, and illustrates again that it is in the lower courts where the problems lie. In both courts there was a tendency for first offenders to be represented more often than women with previous convictions: in the magistrates' courts, 61 per cent of first offenders

24

compared with 72 per cent of other women were unrepresented; in the higher courts the corresponding proportions were 2 per cent and 23 per cent.

TABLE 5

Legal Representation of First Offenders

	Total		Represented		Not Represented		Representation not known	
	No.	%	*No.*	%	*No.*	%	*No.*	%
Magistrates' Courts								
Sentenced to imprisonment	10	100	3	30	7	70	—	—
Untried remands not subsequently imprisoned	58	100	18	31	23	40	17	29
Convicted remands not subsequently imprisoned	71	100	10	14	55	78	6	8
Imprisoned in default of fine	10	100	—	—	6	60	4	40
Total	149	100	31	21	91	61	27	18
Higher Courts								
Sentenced to imprisonment or Borstal Training	23	100	23	100	—	—	—	—
Remands not subsequently imprisoned	34	100	20	59	1	3	13	38
Total	57	100	43	75	1	2	13	23

(5) *Mothers of dependent children*

When the mother of young children is separated from them by being imprisoned, whether on remand or sentence, the hardship imposed, both on her and on the family, exceeds that of most other cases. Women may be taken straight from court to prison without any warning that this was liable to happen, and once in the prison they can have considerable difficulty in finding out what has happened to their children. Phone calls are forbidden and information is slow to come and secondhand when it does. The effect on a family of the sudden removal of the mother in this kind of circumstance is serious, and there are strong arguments against it, both on grounds of family welfare and of cost.[5] Legal assistance can at least ensure that before a mother is remanded in custody or sentenced, all the relevant facts and arguments will be presented to the courts.

A total of 124 women, 20 per cent of the sample, were at the time they were sent to prison, caring for dependent children aged sixteen or less: between them they had 253 such children, three-quarters of whom were under eleven, and 44 per cent under five years of age. The higher courts dealt with forty-seven of these mothers; forty were represented, five were not, and for two there was no information; custodial sentences were imposed in twenty-

25

seven of these cases, including four where the mother was not represented. Magistrates' courts dealt with seventy-seven mothers: sixteen were represented (21 per cent), forty-four (57 per cent) were not, and for the rest there was no information. Twenty-one mothers—sixteen of them unrepresented—were sentenced to imprisonment by the lower courts; the case of one of them is outlined below, and shows how the lack of representation meant the court was sentencing the woman in ignorance of important facts about her.

Case 090
A respectable thirty-six year old married woman with no previous convictions, the mother of two children aged six and nine. The younger one suffered from a serious illness which the mother, under medical supervision, was treating at home. Her husband was a compulsive gambler and as a result the family was in severe financial difficulties and faced with eviction. The mother had a history of mental illness and was currently seriously depressed.

One day when out shopping with her children she stole a number of articles (total value £4) for some of which she seemed to have no use. She was charged, and granted overnight bail. When she appeared in court the next morning she pleaded guilty but said nothing at all on her own behalf. She was sentenced to three months imprisonment. She had spoken to no lawyer, nor were social enquiries made; her home circumstances were not known to the court as she had not told the police about them. She was taken straight from court to prison.

Had this woman been represented a solicitor could have brought the background of the case to the court's attention and it seems unlikely that she would then have been sentenced to imprisonment. Later, she got legal aid for an appeal and was put on probation.

In forty-seven cases, mothers were remanded in custody and not subsequently imprisoned by the lower courts; only four had been represented at the hearing at which they were sent to prison. The majority of these women were remanded for post-conviction enquiries, usually medical; most came from stable homes and had been successfully trusted on bail by the police before their court appearance. A higher rate of representation might well have resulted in more of these mothers being bailed for the medical enquiries; the women themselves were unable to argue this point, since very few were aware that medical examinations could be carried out on bail. The extent

26

to which some defendants were handicapped by the lack of an advocate is illustrated in the following example where, because the mother failed to put her own case, the arguments in favour of bail remained unknown to the court. Although the Widgery Committee did not recommend that legal aid should be granted for bail applications, the survey showed that defendants' lack of representation not infrequently meant that magistrates had to take decisions on the use of custody in the absence of adequate information.

Case 201
A mentally subnormal woman of twenty-nine, married and living with three children between the ages of four and eight. She was given support by the local mental welfare service, and seemed to cope adequately with her family. She had no previous convictions.

One day, on which everything had gone wrong, she decided she could cope no longer: she put the children to bed, broke into her own meter for money and took a train into the country. After a long walk she gave herself up to the police.

The police returned her to her home town, and she was charged with stealing from her meter. She appeared in court but could make little sense of the proceedings. 'I couldn't hear what they said ... a lot of mumbles ... I couldn't think what to say'.

She was remanded in custody for medical reports for two weeks, and her three children were taken into care. The medical report advised that she should return home and resume her contacts with the mental health services.

Had this woman been represented, her solicitor could have explained her situation to the court, pointed out that she had three young children, and that the local mental health service had full information about her, and had been helping her over the years. It is not likely that she would in that case have been sent to prison for medical reports; if the court had wanted such reports, they could have been furnished on bail.

(6) *Those who denied guilt*
Obviously the problems of appearing in court unrepresented were worse for those who believed themselves to be innocent. The great majority of the women tried before the magistrates courts— 76 per cent—pleaded guilty: in the higher courts, the proportion of undefended cases was much lower—46 per cent. The following table shows the position and the extent to which women pleading guilty and not guilty were represented: 43 women who were tried in magistrates' courts but committed for sentence to Quarter Sessions are here included among the magistrates' court cases.

TABLE 6

Pleas and Legal Representation at Court of Trial

Tried at Magistrates' Courts	Total		Represented		Unrepresented		Not known whether represented	
	No.	%	No.	%	No.	%	No.	%
Pleaded guilty	403	100	53	13	315	78	35	9
Pleaded not guilty	58	100	26	45	25	43	7	12
Pleaded both*	10		6		4		—	
Plea not known	56		8		22		26	
Total	527	100	93	17	366	70	68	13
Tried at Higher Courts								
Pleaded guilty	45	100	36	80	6	13	3	7
Pleaded not guilty	38	100	30	79	1	3	7	18
Pleaded both*	2		2		—		—	
Plea not known	11		8		—		3	
Total	96	100	76	79	7	7	13	14

*Women facing more than one charge.

Over 40 per cent of the women who pleaded not guilty before the magistrates had no legal assistance; some of them would undoubtedly have fared differently had they been represented. In one case (described on p. 57) the matter was put right on appeal, although not until the defendant had been committed to prison. In another case the helpfulness of a prison officer remedied a wrong conviction; the unrepresented defendant had told the court that she had been inside Holloway on the date of the alleged offence, but her evidence was not accepted; when she came to prison, an officer checked the records for her, confirmed that she was right, and notified the court accordingly.

The incidence of contested cases is not a full measure of the extent to which the women needed legal help with their defence, for such help may be as necessary at an earlier stage—the stage at which it is decided what plea to make. One of the unexpected findings of the survey was the number of women tried by magistrates' courts who pleaded guilty, or said that they were going to, but who denied when interviewed that they had committed an offence. Among the women tried at the higher courts such cases were rare.

Therefore in trying to gauge the need for legal help in the lower courts, not only the pleas but also the women's accounts of their offences needed to be examined. When this was done it was found that there were two groups who seemed to be in need of legal help; first were 106 women who when interviewed denied having committed any offence at all; two-thirds of these (seventy) were unrepresented. Secondly, there were twenty-two women (ten unrepresented) who when interviewed said that although they supposed they were legally or technically guilty, they nevertheless felt themselves to be morally innocent of the charges : examples included girls who pleaded guilty to larceny but who said that they had not intended to keep the goods. Adding these groups together, there was a total of 128 women who, on account of their denial of guilt, seemed to need some degree of legal help with their defence; over 60 per cent had none. If this index of need is used, the number of persons found to need legal help is considerably greater, and the proportion getting it is less, than if the plea alone is taken into account, for the number of women pleading not guilty in the lower courts was fifty-eight, of whom 45 per cent were unrepresented. These figures illustrate not only the extent to which the women needed help with their defence, but the importance of making it available before defendants are asked to plead.

NOTES

1. Not many women in the sample fell into that category, but an example was a professional woman, who was arrested with others at a political demonstration. She appeared in court with the others, unrepresented, and was remanded in custody untried. When asked by the interviewer why bail had not been allowed, she said she did not know. She knew the police had opposed it, but said that all she heard was a policeman saying that the reason was 'the same as before'. It had not occurred to her to ask in court what the reason was.

2. This widespread ignorance among the unrepresented seems not to have been taken into account in some of the provisions of the Criminal Justice Act 1967. Section 18 of the Act, which was designed to reduce the number of persons remanded in custody, requires magistrates' courts which refuse bail to give the defendant written reasons for so doing, and to inform him of his right to apply for bail to a high court judge. The Home Office explanatory circular to the courts has said that for bail to be 'refused' it has first to be asked for. The effect of this is to deprive those who are not sufficiently versed in court procedure to ask for bail, from benefitting from the new provision. Bottomley, A. K. reported ('New Society' 10.4.69) that in his study of remand prisoners, less than half of those remanded in custody had ever asked for bail.

3. 35% of the unrepresented women were sentenced without such reports – see Section 5.

4. Throughout this report, the phrases 'women with no previous convictions' and 'first offenders' are used to mean women who had no convictions of any kind from the age of 17.

5. The average cost of maintaining a prisoner was in 1967 £14.14.0. a week and the cost of maintaining a child in care averaged £6.4.0. The survey showed that when mothers were sent to prison (on remand or otherwise) a quarter of their dependent children had to be taken into care.

4. INCONSISTENT PLEADERS

Of the 527 women tried at magistrates' courts, 106 when they were interviewed denied having committed any offence.[1] Of these 106 women fifty-six (53 per cent) pleaded guilty, forty-seven (44 per cent) pleaded not guilty, and for three the plea was not known. For convenience, the fifty-six women who pleaded guilty are referred to as 'inconsistent pleaders'.

That more than half of those who claimed to be innocent should plead guilty before the magistrates seemed a surprising finding. How much reliance could be placed on the women's accounts? The interviewers had no reason to believe that those who denied guilt but pleaded guilty were less reliable in their accounts than those who denied guilt and pleaded not guilty, but in neither case was there, as a rule, any way of checking the circumstances of the alleged offences. In spite of this, it seemed worth looking seriously at the fact that so many of those who maintained they were innocent, yet pleaded guilty, for what these women were saying was consistent with evidence from other sources,[2] and few people who have worked in courts or with offenders will be unfamiliar with cases of this sort.

Certain criticisms which some women made of the police are relevant to this subject, and it has not been easy to decide the best way to handle this material. As the prisoners had been guaranteed that the interviews would be confidential, it was impossible to approach the police for information in these cases without revealing what had been alleged. Without any means of checking the truth of what the women said, there were only two alternatives: one was to omit all material relating unfavourably to the police, the other was to report it, while pointing out that the information was derived from only one of the two interested parties. Despite the obvious objections, it was considered right to follow this second course; the subject seemed too important to omit, and weight was also given to the fact that similar allegations were made by a number of the women, and that other people have drawn attention to the same problem. Nevertheless, it should be emphasized that where quotations are given from the women's accounts of police conduct, it is only one side of the story which is available for quotation.

What makes people plead guilty to offences they deny? The fifty-six women who did this, or said that they were going to — nine were interviewed before they pleaded — gave various reasons: seventeen said they were pleading guilty in response to police advice or pressure; eight, including several charged with soliciting and drunkenness, said that there was no point in defending a case where it was only 'my word against the police'; five women said they had pleaded guilty to avoid remands, and another five had done so out of fear that a plea of not guilty meant a harsher sentence. The remaining women gave a variety of different reasons; one simply said she had not got the 'guts' to stand up in court and put her case.

In order to throw some more light on those who denied the offence, yet pleaded guilty, a comparison was made, over all the items of information collected, between the forty-seven consistent and fifty-six inconsistent pleaders who denied their guilt. The inconsistent group were somewhat younger, but apart from this there were no significant differences in social or medical background. There were, however, three main ways in which the two groups differed. The first related to the type of offence : the incidence of public disorder offences like soliciting and drunkenness was higher among the inconsistent, while property offences were more common among the consistent. The table below shows the position.

TABLE 7

Offences of 103 women, tried by magistrates, who on interview denied guilt

| | Plea | |
| | Not Guilty | Guilty |
Offence	No.	No.
Larceny and false pretences	22	10
Receiving	2	6
Soliciting	9	18
Brothel keeping	—	5
Drunkenness	2	8
Drugs	3	2
Other	9	7
Total	47	56

The second difference was that the consistent group, no doubt because of their plea, were remanded untried in custody much more often, thereby lending some justification to the inconsistent pleaders

31

who said they would rather plead guilty and 'have done with it' than risk the remands that go with a defended case. Of the women who denied guilt sixty-two first came to prison after conviction, and forty-seven of them (76 per cent) had pleaded guilty; on the other hand, among the forty-one who denied guilt and first came to prison on untried remand, only a minority of nine (22 per cent) pleaded inconsistently. Thirdly, there was a marked difference in the representation of the two groups. Seventy-eight of the women who denied guilt had no legal advice before pleading, and two-thirds of them (fifty-two) pleaded guilty, but among the twenty-two women who were known to have had legal help before pleading, the proportion pleading inconsistently was 13 per cent—three women.[3] Does this mean that legal advice reduces inconsistent pleading? It can be argued that such a conclusion is not warranted, because in the lower courts those who are represented are likely to be those who are most determined to defend themselves: they do not plead not guilty because they are represented, rather, they are represented because they intend to plead not guilty. However, in the higher courts a different situation exists; virtually all who are sent for trial have legal assistance, irrespective of their wish to defend themselves, and the survey showed that in the high court trial cases inconsistent pleading was as rare as it was among the represented women in the lower courts: of thirty-three women tried in the higher courts who, when interviewed, mantained their innocence, five (15 per cent) pleaded guilty. Thus there does appear to be some evidence that in a group of defendants who have access to legal advice before pleading, few of those who believe themselves to be innocent will plead guilty.[4]

Perhaps the most disturbing feature about the inconsistent pleaders was the number of women among them who had no previous convictions. There were, among the cases tried by magistrates, twenty-four women without previous convictions who, when they were interviewed, denied having committed any offence: fourteen of them, nearly 60 per cent, pleaded guilty. Two said they had done so in order to avoid remands, and one—the only represented woman, whose case is the last in the third footnote on page 37—said her solicitor had told her to plead guilty. One girl who was remanded untried on a charge of possessing drugs said that the police had planted these on her; after much hesitation she decided not to say so in court, as she felt such an accusation would prejudice the bench against her.[5] The majority of the inconsistent first offenders, nine of the fourteen, gave police advice or pressure as their reason for pleading guilty. Some of them said that the police had threatened that they would be 'sent down' if they pleaded not guilty; others said that they had been told that they would 'get off' (with a fine or probation etc.) if they did not contest the case. Several girls said that they had been advised to plead guilty in a kindly, even fatherly spirit, the policemen telling them that this was the simplest way to get the case over, and to avoid the risk of publicity, or remands in custody. It was easy to see how those without experience of police stations or courts might gratefully accept such advice, and it was significant that while only 9 per cent of inconsistent recidivists gave police advice as their reason for pleading guilty, 64 per cent of the inconsistent first offenders said they had done so in response to police persuasion.

Table 7 showed that certain kinds of offence were particularly associated with inconsistent pleas, soliciting being the outstanding case. Fifty-nine girls—all but one unrepresented—were charged with this offence; twenty-seven denied it but eighteen of them pleaded guilty. All but two of these eighteen girls admitted that they were prostitutes: what they denied was that they had at the time of arrest been plying their trade. Five of the nine women who pleaded not guilty also said the same. All these girls gave similar accounts: when arrested, they had been out in the areas where they were known, but not with 'business' in mind; some were walking with girl friends (often other prostitutes), others were talking to boy friends in the street, and one or two were arrested on getting out of cars. One professional—she pleaded not guilty—said she had been stopped on her way by a seaman who asked her to come aboard his ship to 'do business'. She refused and walked on, and was then arrested for soliciting.

The Street Offences Act 1959 undoubtedly puts these girls into a difficult position. If they have previous convictions or cautions,[6] they become by definition 'common prostitutes', and if a known prostitute is talking on a street corner to a man, the police may well arrest her for soliciting, although the man in fact may be a friend or a stranger asking the way. What is such a girl to do? She can attempt to defend the case but to do so effectively she needs as a witness the person she was talking to. A young girl of eighteen gave an account of the difficulties. She was arrested for soliciting, and remanded in custody when she pleaded not guilty. She did not ask for legal aid, nor did the court suggest it. When interviewed she said that she had been in Piccadilly when a man asked her the way to a club. She directed him, and was then arrested for soliciting. She said that she asked the arresting officer if he would go with her to the club to find the man, and so prove the contents of their conversation, but this was refused. In such circumstances it is not easy for a girl to try and contest the police evidence, and without legal advice and assistance it must be virtually impossible.

33

There may be little sympathy for the professional who is arrested when off duty, but the present legal position, which exposes persons with previous convictions or cautions for soliciting to the repeated risk of wrongful arrest, seems unsatisfactory. The women themselves generally accepted the situation as an inevitable hazard of their trade, and pleaded guilty in a more or less resigned kind of way: this, no doubt, explained the very low rate of representation. However, one might speculate what would be the outcome if an experiment similar to that described by Donald Goff[7] were tried with London prostitutes. Goff reported that in New York City, where public drunkenness is not an offence, alcoholics were habitually charged with 'disorderly conduct': they were never represented, cases were rarely defended and almost 100 per cent were sentenced to short stays in the workhouse. As an experiment, counsel was assigned to some 1400 cases—to argue the legal point that drunkenness did not necessarily constitute disorderly conduct. Only seven of the 1400 represented people were found guilty. It would be interesting to know what proportion of girls charged with soliciting would be found guilty, if they were represented on this scale.

Whilst sixteen of the eighteen inconsistent prostitutes admitted their trade, there were two girls aged eighteen and nineteen who pleaded guilty although they denied that they had ever solicited in their lives. Neither had a previous conviction of any kind. One said that the police told her that if she pleaded guilty she would have 'a better chance of getting off'. She added 'They say that to everyone but I didn't know that then'. The case of the other is outlined below.

Case 591
A nineteen year old girl with no previous convictions who was mixing with criminal friends. She had been cautioned for soliciting although she denied (to the probation officer, as well as to two different interviewers in the present enquiry) that she had ever done this. On the day of her arrest she was walking with a known prostitute and both were charged. She said that the police threatened her with a remand in custody if she did not plead guilty. 'I was frightened and wanted to get it over with'. She pleaded guilty and was then remanded in custody for medical enquiries. Until she reached Holloway she was ignorant of the nature of legal aid. 'I thought it was something needed for Quarter Sessions only'.

In two other types of offence particularly associated with inconsistent pleading—receiving and brothel keeping—the defendants' need for advice on the legal implications of the charge emerged very clearly. Six women who pleaded guilty to charges of receiving said when interviewed, that they had not known until the police told them, that the goods were stolen; none of them seemed to be aware that this could be a defence to the charge and none of them had legal advice. Similarly, the five women (all unrepresented) who denied that they had engaged in brothel keeping, yet pleaded guilty to the charge, did not appreciate the legal elements in the offence. It may seem quite unbelievable to the ordinary person that someone who believes herself to be innocent of brothel-keeping (or soliciting) can plead guilty to such an offence, yet the evidence was that a defendant may do so if she believes such a plea to be a lesser evil than the others she feels threatened with. A woman with no previous convictions, the mother of four young children, admitted when interviewed that she was promiscuous, but wholly denied any experience of prostitution or brothel keeping. On being charged with the latter, she said that she had been told at the police station that the quickest way to get the thing over and return to her children would be to plead guilty, and she did so. Once remanded to Holloway (for medical reports) she sought legal aid, and tried, without success, to change her plea. Another woman with no previous convictions pleaded guilty to brothel keeping although she denied it; she said that the police had told her it was unnecessary to contact a lawyer, since a contested case would only involve scandal and publicity, whilst a plea of guilty would enable her to be out of court within five minutes.

Whatever weight may be put on the women's accounts in these cases, the point which repeatedly emerged was the importance to the accused person of having legal advice before pleading. Although in open court the defendant is asked whether she understands the charge, and is given the opportunity to put her case, the findings suggest that this is not enough: the person who has become persuaded that she is 'legally' guilty, or that it is to her advantage to plead guilty to a charge she denies, has made her decisions before she appears in court.

Conclusions

It appeared that in the lower courts inconsistent pleading is a major problem, stemming in part from the lack of legal advice. Two-thirds of the unrepresented women who maintained that they were innocent nevertheless pleaded guilty, while among those who were represented, whether in the higher or lower courts, the percentage pleading inconsistently was not more than 15 per cent.

A contributory factor in inconsistent pleading appeared to be a tendency for the police to persuade defendants to plead guilty, although it should be emphasized that only a minority of prisoners mentioned this: of 139 women in the sample who said that they were innocent, 18 per cent (twenty-six) said that the police had tried to persuade them to plead guilty;[8] while of the fifty-six women who pleaded guilty in magistrates' courts although they said they were innocent, less than a third (seventeen) gave police persuasion as the reason. Nevertheless, among those who denied guilt and mentioned police persuasion, the majority—seventeen of twenty-six—pleaded guilty, the proportion being highest among first offenders.

The problem is not a new one; the Law Society, in their evidence to the 1962 Royal Commission on the Police, said that 'advice to plead guilty is too readily given by police officers' and suggested that the police should never discuss the plea with an accused person.[9] The evidence of the National Association of Probation Officers also drew attention to the problem:— 'A serious complaint commonly met by probation officers, and which we are convinced has substantial foundation, is that when questioning suspected offenders the police may offer to "put in a good word" or indicate that a lenient treatment might be suggested in court if the offender will admit the offence ... and plead guilty. This may happen when the offender is not clearly aware of the nature of the charge against him, and (may) ... lead ... to a conviction of an offence more serious than that on which a verdict would have been sought (or easy to obtain) in a contested case. We have no doubt from the strength of the evidence of our members that the practice ... does take place, however subtly it may be employed.'[10] The Royal Commission accepted the evidence on this, and said that the practice should be 'firmly checked by Chief Constables'.

Since the problem still exists, what could be done? A number of suggestions have been made in the context of a similar abuse also discussed by the Royal Commission—the use by the police of undesirable methods of obtaining statements and confessions. One of these is that independent persons, such as magistrates or solicitors should be present at the police interrogation.[11] Inconsistent pleading, whether in response to police persuasion or other causes, would certainly diminish if it could be ensured that every accused person had the chance of speaking to a legal adviser before the plea is entered. In effect, this is what happens in the cases tried before the higher courts where inconsistent pleading was not a significant problem. If the same happened in the lower courts, it would not only ensure that any person who had been influenced by police persuasion would have easy access to independent advice; it would also ensure that before a defendant entered the dock, he would have had expert advice as to the nature of the charge, and as to the need of legal assistance in facing it.

NOTES

1. The 527 women included 43 tried by the lower courts and then committed for sentence. The 106 women were those who denied any kind of guilt; they do not include the 'technically guilty' referred to on p. 29 nor do they include those who denied some offences while admitting to others.

2. See Royal Commission on the Police 1962, Cmnd. 1728, paras. 369 and 372; also Minutes of Evidence, pp. 1221 and 1077; and 'The Prosecution Process in England and Wales' by Justice, 1970, pp 5-8. See also Clive Davies' 'Innocents in Jail', 'New Society' 6 Nov. 1969, p. 742.

3. Their cases were of some interest. One was a drug offence of the 'absolute' kind, the girl alleging that she did not know that the drugs were on her premises. Possibly in view of later interpretations of the law, such a case would to-day be defended. The second case was that of a prostitute, accused of assaulting and robbing a client. She denied the charge, and said she would plead not guilty. When visited by a solicitor in prison, it seems that she was told that the charge would be reduced to one of larceny if she pleaded guilty, and this is what she did, presumably in order to avoid months in custody awaiting trial at the Old Bailey.

The last case was that of a middle-aged book-keeper, a woman of good character: she was accused of falsifying accounts, and larceny thereby. She admitted that she had done the former in order to balance the books, but denied that she had ever profited from it. She said that her solicitor had nevertheless told her to plead guilty, on the grounds that it would shorten the proceedings.

This last case—the only one of its kind in the sample—raised the question of how far lawyers may also persuade defendants to plead inconsistently. Justice, in its 1970 report on 'Complaints against Lawyers' says that such complaints are made, but it is clearly not easy to distinguish cases where the advice to plead guilty is given on legal grounds, in the client's best interest, from cases where it may be given for unworthy reasons.

4. If this is so, better legal aid arrangements in the lower courts may be expected to lead to an increase in the proportion of defendants who plead not guilty. This may well be the reason why the growth of legal aid in the higher courts has been accompanied by a rise in the proportion of defended cases. The Beeching Commission did not consider this possibility. (Royal Commission on Assizes and Quarter Sessions, 1966-1969 Cmnd. 4153, paras. 410 and 411.)

5. This point was put to the Royal Commission on the Police by the Society of Labour Lawyers, p. 1315 of the Evidence: 'An accused person who has reason to complain of the conduct of the police finds himself in a very difficult position. If he instructs his solicitor . . . to put forward his complaints, he does so at his peril since magistrates and judges are thought to be prejudiced against accused persons who . . . make complaints against the police. Moreover, there is seldom independent evidence to support complaints . . .'.

The same point is made by Justice: 'If there are indications of police malpractice . . . the barrister has to consider very carefully whether or not to risk incurring the hostility of the trial judge.' (Complaints against Lawyers, Appendix B).

6. The Street Offences Act 1959 enables women who are cautioned to apply for the caution to be expunged by a magistrates' court; few girls seemed aware of the procedure and only one reported that she had tried to use it; she said that when she went to a police station for this purpose, she was told she needed to have the number of the officer who cautioned her, and she did not have it.

7. The Drunkenness Offence, ed. Cook, T., Gath, D., and Hensman, C. Pergamon Press 1969, pp. 89–95.

8. There was no evidence that complaints about police pressure to plead guilty came more frequently from those held in police custody, nor did such women plead guilty in response to the alleged pressure more often that did those who had been allowed police bail.

9. Royal Commission on the Police 1962. Minutes of Evidence p. 1077

10. Royal Commission on the Police 1962. Minutes of Evidence p. 1221.

11. See Jackson, R. M. 'Enforcing the Law'. 1967, pp. 71–8. Also 'Justice': 'The Interrogation of Suspects', 1967.

5. HOW FAR ARE SOCIAL ENQUIRY REPORTS A SUBSTITUTE?

The importance and value to the courts of obtaining background information on offenders before sentencing them, was emphasized by the Streatfeild Committee:[1] the information is supplied by probation officers in the form of social enquiry reports, the purpose of which is to assist the court, by describing the offender's circumstances and home surroundings, to determine the most suitable way of dealing with the case.

To what extent, if any, do social enquiry reports obviate the need for the defendant to be legally represented? Can it be argued that the court's possession of background information about the offender renders legal assistance to him less necessary?

A number of points are relevant. The first is the scale on which social enquiry reports are prepared. Although this part of probation work has increased substantially in recent years, social enquiry reports are still only provided in a small proportion of all cases coming before the courts. In 1968, for example, when the number of full social enquiry reports made on adults was 101,700,[2] the number of adults prosecuted for non motoring offences was 564,000.

Among a sample of prisoners, one would expect the proportion of cases with reports to be higher, and in the present survey, social enquiry reports were known to have been made on 324 of the 587 women found guilty, i.e. on 55 per cent. A third of the convicted women (198) were sentenced without reports: this proportion was similar in lower and higher court cases, but there was a big difference between the courts in the extent to which those who were without reports were also without legal assistance. In the following table it will be seen that 2 per cent of the high court cases, but a quarter of those from the magistrates' courts (114 of 463) were both unrepresented and without reports. Inevitably, where no social enquiry reports were called for, and where the defendant was also unrepresented, the courts were liable to pass sentence in the absence of adequate information.

38

TABLE 8
Social Enquiry Reports and Legal Representation*

Magistrates' Courts	Total		Social Enquiry Reports				Not known whether made	
			Reports made		Not made			
	No.	%	No.	%	No.	%	No.	%
Represented	73	100	43	59	23	31	7	10
Unrepresented	326	100	180	55	114	35	32	10
Representation not known	64		25		25		14	
Total	463	100	248	54	162	35	53	11
Higher Courts								
Represented	92	100	55	60	29	31	8	9
Unrepresented	20	100	17	85	3	15	—	—
Representation not known	12		4		4		4	
Total	124	100	76	61	36	29	12	10

*The table excludes 36 women who were acquitted.

Among the 114 women whom the lower courts sentenced without reports or representation were twenty-four first offenders, six of whom were imprisoned. Eighty-one women altogether were sentenced to imprisonment by the lower courts : 58 per cent of them (forty-seven) were sentenced without social enquiry reports, 80 per cent (sixty-five) without being represented, and 46 per cent (thirty-seven) were imprisoned without reports or representation. In the higher courts, of forty-nine women sentenced to imprisonment, seven were unrepresented, twenty-two were sentenced without reports, but only two had neither reports nor legal assistance.

The proportion of cases sentenced to imprisonment without social enquiry reports is probably lower now than it was in 1967, since Home Office Circulars were issued in 1968[3] advising both lower and higher courts to obtain reports before sentencing any woman to imprisonment. It would be interesting to know to what extent this advice has been followed; an earlier circular, addressed to the higher courts only[4] had recommended that pre-trial social enquiry reports should be furnished for certain specified categories of offenders. In the present survey one hundred and eleven of the higher court cases came within these categories, but in one third of them, social enquiry reports had not been made.

The 197 unrepresented women on whom probation reports were made were certainly better off than the 117 who were both unrepresented and without reports: before sentencing the former, the courts would at least have information on the social background of the case. But the presence of a probation officer did not necessarily compensate for the absence of a defence lawyer, for the functions of the two are different and intended to serve a different purpose. The probation officer is an officer of the court and may advise as to the most suitable sentence to be imposed; for example, the officer who considers, in the light of his experience and knowledge, that Borstal training or imprisonment is the most suitable disposal for an offender, will advise the court accordingly. In 80 per cent of the 324 cases where social enquiry reports were made, the research workers were able to see them, and learn what, if anything had been recommended by the probation officers. For twenty-two girls a Borstal sentence was advised and for three women a prison sentence was recommended. In these cases there seemed to be a particular need for a defence lawyer to put the opposing arguments; but fourteen of these twenty-five prisoners were unrepresented, and in the event eight of the fourteen were sent to Borstal or prison. The helplessness and isolation of some of these women may be illustrated by the following case :

Case 416

An eighteen-year-old girl with one conviction for larceny, was charged with breach of probation because she repeatedly ran away from probation homes. Her probation officer recommended that she should be sent to Borstal, and she was committed for sentence.

She was unrepresented at both higher and lower court. She hoped that her parents would come to Quarter Sessions to speak for her, but she was given so little notice of the date of hearing that this could not be arranged. In court the Recorder asked her if she had any friend who could speak for her and she named the probation officer.

A Borstal sentence was imposed.

A similar situation exists when, on the advice of a probation officer, punitive remands are imposed; these were cases where the probation officer recommended a remand in custody on the grounds that it might have the effect of bringing a girl 'to her senses'. Generally the girls concerned had been on probation and had breached it once or more. The following is an example of such a case:

Case 176

A seventeen-year-old girl, with no previous findings of guilt, was convicted of shoplifting some groceries: a supervision order had been made on her a year earlier, when she ran away from home.

She was bailed for a social enquiry report to be made. The report, after describing the home background, added 'It could be that a period on remand in Holloway would have a salutary effect on her, and that she would be more willing to co-operate after that.'

She was remanded in custody for three weeks, for medical reports.

The use of remands in custody for penal purposes is understandable, though debatable: what seemed quite clear was that an unrepresented girl, who did not understand court or bail procedures, could have no hope of effectively opposing such a remand. A solicitor could have pressed the arguments for allowing the reports to be made on bail and could, if necessary, have applied for bail to a judge in chambers.

Another way in which probation officers have obviously to act towards their 'clients' in a manner markedly different from the defence solicitor, is when proceedings are taken for breach of probation; in effect the probation officer has then to act as the prosecution, it being on his initiative that the accused is brought back to court and exposed to the risk of being sent to prison, on remand or otherwise. Of seventy-eight women who entered the sample on charges of breach of probation, only twenty were represented. Of the seventy-eight, thirty-two were imprisoned, seventeen without being represented. Of course on such occasions the probation officer's report will be fair and comprehensive, but he cannot fulfil the function of a defence lawyer, when that is not his role.

These examples illustrate some of the differences between their roles which make it difficult to regard the probation officer as a substitute for the defence lawyer. A fundamental difference of another kind arises from the fact that the probation officer's report is only used by the court after the issue of guilt has been decided. It is not part of a probation officer's function to advise accused persons about the proceedings, or about the plea: and an officer cannot be of assistance to the unrepresented defendant who wishes to contest the charges, or who does not understand them. On the evidence of the present sample, the time when the accused most needs an independent person to consult, is before her first appearance in court, and the time she most needs someone to speak for her is at that appearance: it is then that she may be asked to plead and present her case, and it is then that the court takes the decision on whether to remand, and if so whether to grant bail. But although a lawyer can effectively enter the scene at this stage, probation officers do not. For the women in this sample, the usual procedure was that they were remanded in custody for reports, after the case was heard. It was in prison that they were interviewed by probation officers, and they could not be helped by social enquiry reports, however favourable, until their period in custody had elapsed.

NOTES

1. Report of the Interdepartmental Committee on the Business of the Criminal Courts 1961, Cmnd. 1289 H.M.S.O.
2. Report on the Work of the Probation and After Care Department 1966–1968 Cmnd. 4233, Appendix E.
3. 188/1968 and 189/1968
4. 84/1963.

6. TYPE AND TIME OF LEGAL CONTACT

(1) *Grant and refusal of legal aid*

Magistrates' Courts

In the 484 cases disposed of by magistrates' courts, 305 women (62 per cent) made no attempt to get legal help for their trial. Fourteen women (3 per cent of the total) got legal help privately in the first instance; two women made use of the legal advice scheme and 136 (28 per cent) applied for legal aid. Of these 136 applications fifty-nine were granted (43 per cent) and thirty-three were refused (24 per cent): in the remaining cases the women had returned to court before receiving answers and the research workers' attempts to get information from other sources were unsuccessful. For all those who applied for legal aid and received no answer while in prison, the waiting period was a source of tension and anxiety, —the women daily expecting a letter or solicitor's visit, and dreading lest in the end a brief consultation in the court cells would be their sole contact with their solicitor. The unsatisfactory nature of such hurried conferences was emphasised by all prisoners who experienced them.

The proportion of women known to have been refused legal aid was 24 per cent, but on the assumption that the cases for which information was not obtained were treated no more favourably than the others, the eventual refusal rate must have been about 33 per cent. In 1967, the overall national refusal rate in summary cases for men and women was 23 per cent of all applications,[1] but this national total of applications must have included many trivial cases where there was no question of the defendant being sent to prison, on remand or otherwise, and one might have expected that a sample of prisoners would have a lower rate of refusal. Of the offences for which legal aid was refused 60 per cent were indictable, most of them being property offences.

An important factor in the granting of legal aid was the time when the application was made. The refusal rate to women who applied for legal aid from prison before being tried was 13 per cent, but to those who applied on convicted remand it was 47 per cent. The figures are shown in the following table. It was clear that the courts generally made it their policy to refuse legal aid where it was applied for by a convicted person remanded for enquiries. In fact the time of application seemed to be a more important determining factor in the grant of legal aid than the income of the applicant; a comparison of the incomes of those granted and refused legal aid did not show that the latter were markedly more prosperous.

TABLE 9

Grant and Refusal of Legal Aid According to Time of Application

Time of Application	Total		Legal aid granted		Legal aid refused		Outcome not known	
	No.	%	No.	%	No.	%	No.	%
Before prison or in court	27	100	20	74	6	22	1	4
In prison, untried	55	100	28	51	7	13	20	36
In prison, convicted, but unsentenced	36	100	6	17	17	47	13	36
Other, or not known	18	—	5	—	3	—	10	—
Total	136	100	59	44	33	24	44	32

Very few women used their own resources to get legal help after they were refused legal aid: only four of the thirty-three did so (12 per cent), a lower proportion than that of 33 per cent reported by the Widgery Committee (paragraph 42). It suggests that the legal aid scheme introduced in 1968 under the Criminal Justice Act 1967 may have the effect of reducing the number of legal aid applications from Holloway in magistrates' courts' cases. Under this scheme, defendants are liable to be assessed for contributions after the case is concluded, and on the evidence of this sample, this is an expense few of those seeking legal help felt able or willing to meet.

How were the thirty-three women to whom legal aid was refused dealt with by the courts? One was acquitted, twenty-three were dealt with by non-custodial measures and nine were imprisoned. Since of the eighty-one women imprisoned by magistrates' courts only eighteen applied for legal aid before they were sentenced, this meant that half the applications from women who were sentenced to imprisonment were refused.

The principles on which legal aid are granted or refused are of relatively small importance so long as the majority of prisoners do not apply for it. In the present sample of 484 women sent to prison on sentence or remand by magistrates' courts, more than

44

two thirds (335) were unrepresented. Ten per cent of these were unrepresented because legal aid had been refused, but 90 per cent were unrepresented because they had made no attempt to get assistance, nor had courts invited them to do so. The most recent Criminal Statistics show a similar picture.[2] In 1969, when some 289,000 indictable offences were tried summarily, only 51,000 applications for legal aid in such cases were made. 7,560 of these applications were refused, which means that of some 245,000 defendants who faced indictable charges without legal aid, 3 per cent did so because it had been refused, but 97 per cent did so because they had neither asked for nor been offered it.[3] It is clear which problem is the more serious one, and it is also clear that it will only be overcome if the magistrates' courts make more positive attempts to search out cases needing legal assistance. In 1964, the Lord Chief Justice said in a high court case[4] that it was no answer for a court to say that a defendant had not asked for legal aid: irrespective of the prisoner's application, it was held to be the court's duty to see that any necessary assistance was provided. Unless the legal aid system is administered in the same spirit in the lower courts, large numbers of defendants in need of help will continue to go without it.[5]

Higher Courts

The position was very different from that in the magistrates' courts. First, the proportion applying for legal aid was much greater: of the 139 women dealt with by the higher courts, 104 applied for legal aid, i.e. 73 per cent as against the 28 per cent who applied at the magistrates' courts; seven women obtained private help without applying for legal aid first (5 per cent compared with 3 per cent in the lower courts). Only seventeen women made no attempt to get themselves represented (12 per cent as against 62 per cent of the magistrates' court cases). Secondly, the proportion refused legal aid was much lower than in the magistrates' courts : only five of the 104 applications were rejected, a refusal rate of less than 5 per cent compared with one of 24 per cent in the lower courts. Two of the five women who were refused aid obtained private help, one by means of a dock brief. The three others, all of whom were committed for sentence, remained unrepresented. None of them appeared to have any financial resources—two were living on national assistance. Two of the three were sentenced to imprisonment, one of them, the pregnant mother of a young son, for two years.

As in the magistrates' courts, most of those who were unrepresented had neither requested, nor been offered, legal aid : of the twenty unrepresented women, three had their application rejected, but seventeen had never applied. The Criminal Statistics for 1968 and 1969[6] show that this remains the case. Most of those who are unrepresented, in the higher as in the lower courts, are not refused legal aid. They never apply for it.

The rate of representation was markedly higher among women committed for trial than it was among those committed for sentence: 7 per cent (seven) of the ninety-six trial cases were unrepresented, compared with a third (thirteen) of the forty-three cases committed for sentence. Considering the high risk of imprisonment to those who are committed for sentence, the substantial proportion who were unrepresented was disturbing: in 1967 17 per cent of women's trials resulted in custodial sentences, but 51 per cent of women's committed for sentence were imprisoned or sent to Borstal.[7] The rate of representation among women committed for sentence has probably improved since this survey was carried out but the most recent national figures, which are for men and women together, show that the situation is still unsatisfactory: in 1969, when 65 per cent of those committed for sentence were given custodial sentences, 15 per cent of such defendants (compared with 2 per cent of trial defendants) were unrepresented.[8]

(2) *Stage at which lawyers were consulted*

Of the 184 women who were represented, twenty-five came to Holloway on sentence, without having previously been remanded in custody. The other 159 represented women first came to prison on remand; only 23 per cent of them (thirty-six) had been represented at the hearing at which they were sent to prison; 54 per cent (eighty-six) initially made contact with their lawyers (or lawyer's clerks) in prison, and another 23 per cent (thirty-seven) first met their lawyers after they were released from the remand. These proportions were the same among the higher and lower court cases. How many women contacted solicitors from the police station is not known, but eight said that the police had prevented them from doing so.[9]

Among those who first saw their solicitors after a remand period in prison, were twelve legally aided women whose only contact was a hasty conference in the court cells just before the resumed hearing. These women—seven of whom were sentenced to imprisonment— had all waited in vain for a solicitor's visit in prison, and then found that although they had been granted legal aid, they were not allowed sufficient time with their lawyers to explain the circumstances of their case. It was a cause of much bitterness. Only defendants remanded in custody are liable to be handicapped in this way; those who are bailed can be sure of contacting their solicitors in good time.

The extent to which the women sentenced by the higher courts were represented in the magistrates' courts' proceedings was of some interest. None of the twenty women (thirteen were sentence committals) who were unrepresented before the higher courts had been represented in the lower courts. Of the twenty-seven women who were represented in the higher courts when committed for sentence, only ten had been represented at the trial before the magistrates. Among the seventy-five women who were represented when tried by the higher courts, fifty-eight (77 per cent) had been represented in the preliminary proceedings in the lower court.

Of the eighty-one women sentenced to imprisonment by magistrates' courts, thirteen appealed against sentence. Only one of these appellants had been represented at her trial, but nine were represented for the appeal. Five appellants, none of whom had been represented when sentenced, but all of whom had legal help for the appeal, were successful. In each of these cases it appeared that the sentences would never have been imposed, had the women been represented at the trial and their full circumstances been made known. Yet women sentenced to imprisonment by the lower courts were usually reluctant to appeal, since they were always warned by prison staff of the danger that their sentences (unless already the maximum) might be increased. It is generally held that the fear of an increased sentence will deter only the 'unmeritorious' appellant, and the Court of Appeal, by threatening the unmeritorious with loss of time, operates on this assumption.[10] There was however evidence in the survey that the fear of longer periods in prison deters the meritorious as much as the unmeritorious: however remote the risk (and they cannot assess it) and irrespective of the merits of their case, many women felt unwilling to expose themselves to a possibly unfavourable appeal result.

NOTES

1. Criminal Statistics 1967 Cmnd 3689, Table XVII.
2. Criminal Statistics 1969 Cmnd 4398, Tables I (a) and XVII (a).
3. The Criminal Statistics do not show, for the lower courts, how many of those without legal aid were privately represented. Michael Zander's survey in the Criminal Law Review, Dec. 1969 on 'Unrepresented Defendants in the Criminal Courts' suggests a proportion of some 8%: his was a London sample, covering indictable and non-indictable cases.
4. McAlinden, The Times, 10.3.64.
5. The same conclusions are reached by Borrie, Prof. G. J., and Varcoe, J. R., in their report 'Legal Aid in Criminal Proceedings: a Regional Survey' (Institute of Judicial Administration, University of Birmingham). Their study was carried out in the West Midlands in 1969. An important finding was that courts which granted virtually every legal aid application made, nevertheless failed to suggest to defendants who did not apply, that they should do so—even when the cases were serious, fell within the Widgery criteria, and resulted in custodial sentences.
6. Table XVII (a).
7. Criminal Statistics 1967, Table II (a).
8. Criminal Statistics 1969, Table II (a) and XVII (a).
9. Similar allegations are reported in para. 32 of 'Legal Aid in Criminal Proceedings: a Regional Survey' by Borrie, Prof. G. J. and Varcoe, J. R.
10. The Times Law Report, 17.3.1970: the Lord Chief Justice, in threatening hopeless appellants with loss of time, said that 'The object is to enable prompt attention to be given to meritorious cases by deterring the unmeritorious applications that stand in their way.'

Who are the unrepresented? Do they differ socially, criminally, or in other ways from those who have lawyers? If any attempt is to be made to improve the legal services to prisoners, an answer to this question is needed. Comparisons were therefore made between the represented and unrepresented women, over all the available information. Attention is drawn only to differences that were significant at the 5 per cent level.

Higher Courts

Of the 139 women sentenced by the higher courts, 102 were represented, (74 per cent), twenty were not (14 per cent), and for seventeen information was not available.

All the unrepresented women were dealt with at Quarter Sessions, no Assize cases being unrepresented.

The twenty unrepresented women were a distinct group, differing from the represented in that they were mostly young girls (ten were under twenty-one) with several previous convictions, who had been on probation unsuccessfully, and were now committed for sentence. In social characteristics they were more isolated, more often homeless and unemployed than the represented women. Their plea was the only other distinguishing factor: thirty-two of the represented pleaded not guilty (31 per cent) but only one of the twenty unrepresented girls did so (5 per cent).

Magistrates' Courts

Of the 484 cases dealt with by the lower courts, eighty-two were represented (17 per cent) 335 were not (69 per cent) and for sixty-seven there was no information.

When the represented and unrepresented women were compared, the latter emerged, as far as their social background was concerned, as the women with least to lose: more of them were homeless (21 per cent compared with 9 per cent) or in temporary accommodation; fewer of them were in touch with their families (31 per cent compared with 50 per cent) and a lower proportion was married

(13 per cent compared with 22 per cent). More of the represented received their income from national assistance (26 per cent as compared with 14 per cent) which in the present sample reflected a relatively stable way of life, since to qualify for assistance it is necessary to have an address; (also of course, it makes it easier for a court to judge whether legal aid is justified on financial grounds.)

There was a tendency for the Irish and Scots to be represented less often than others: 12 per cent of the unrepresented were Scots, as compared with 3 per cent of the represented; while the Irish accounted for 17 per cent of the unrepresented, but only for 6 per cent of the represented. Part of the explanation was that the Scots and Irish prisoners were proportionately more often involved in public disorder offences, particularly drunkenness and malicious damage, for which the rate of representation was very low.

At first sight, age was not a significant factor in representation. But on examination it was found that this was because contrary trends among remanded and sentenced prisoners were cancelling each other out. On the one hand, the women who were imprisoned without previous remands were as a group considerably older than those who were remanded, and were seldom represented. On the other hand, among the remands it was the older women who were more often represented than the young girls.

A comparison of the mental and physical health of the represented and unrepresented showed only one significant difference, the higher incidence of alcoholism among the unrepresented (14 per cent compared with 1 per cent). This was because the majority of alcoholics were fine defaulters, who were never represented.

Information about social class, as measured by the father's occupation, was rather sketchy but it did not appear to discriminate between the represented and unrepresented groups, nor did any other significant differences in the women's backgrounds emerge.

The criminal records showed that first offenders were a little more likely to be represented than those with previous convictions: 27 per cent of the former, as compared with 17 per cent of the latter, had legal assistance. This finding may be welcome to those who hold what the Widgery Committee described as the widespread view that 'public money should not be devoted to the repeated defence of persistent criminals' (paragraph 167).

The rate of representation, with three exceptions, varied little with the nature of the offence, or with the values involved. The 484 magistrates' court cases were distributed among the various offences in the following proportions: 36 per cent larceny (including 15 per cent shoplifting), 14 per cent soliciting or brothel

49

keeping, 9 per cent drunkenness, 9 per cent drugs, 8 per cent false pretences, 5 per cent breaking, 5 per cent breach of probation without fresh offence, 3 per cent violence (including child cruelty); the remaining 11 per cent were mainly assorted non indictable offences. The proportions represented were similar in all types of offence, except for prostitution and drunkeness where the rate of representation was very low (2 per cent), and drug cases, where it was exceptionally high—44 per cent; this undoubtedly reflected the fact that all the women charged with drugs offences had been remanded before trial, on bail or in custody, for drug analysis, and this gave them time to seek help.

As in the higher courts, a significant difference between the represented and unrepresented women lay in their plea: 35 per cent of the represented, compared with 8 per cent of the un-represented, pleaded not guilty to some or all of the charges. Inconsistent pleading was closely related to representation, as was seen in Section 4 : among the represented it was rare, but among the unrepresented almost three times as many women as pleaded not guilty maintained that they were innocent.

The biggest difference between the represented and unrepresented lay in the proportions who had been remanded in custody before trial: 60 per cent of the former, as compared with 19 per cent of the latter. Table 1 showed how different groups of prisoners had different rates of representation; among fine defaulters it was nil, and among those sentenced to imprisonment it was 17 per cent; while among those not given custodial sentences it was 35 per cent for the untried remands, and 12 per cent for those remanded after conviction. That the fine defaulters and imprisoned women were so seldom represented reflected the type of offender given such sentences; in the main these were older women, recidivists who had often been in prison before. Prostitution, shoplifting and drunkenness figured prominently among their offences. Although one might have thought that such women, being experienced in court procedure and knowing that prison sentences were a likely risk, would make the maximum use of legal aid facilities, the opposite was true; the majority had never considered getting legal help, even when they denied their offence.

That the women remanded before trial had so much higher a rate of representation than those remanded after conviction was interesting, for the two groups were very similar in most respects, such as age, background, health, and number of previous convictions. Only two distinguishing features emerged. One related to the offence; the convicted remands were more often charged with public disorder offences (22 per cent compared with 8 per cent) and shoplifting (19 per cent compared with 6 per cent) while

50

among the untried women there was a higher incidence of drugs cases (20 per cent compared with 4 per cent). Connected with these differences in offence was a difference in the proportions pleading not guilty: 25 per cent of the untried women, compared with 4 per cent of the convicted, pleaded not guilty. This however did not account for the difference in representation, since the untried women had a higher rate of representation in both defended and undefended cases, and were indeed more frequently represented on pleas of guilty than convicted women were on pleas of not guilty.

Probably the most important reason for the differences in the representation of the two groups was what happened to them when they got to court the morning after arrest (only 1 per cent of the whole sample was summonsed). The untried group were remanded to prison before their cases were heard. The reason for adjournment was not known in all cases, but not many women were remanded because they asked to be represented : lack of time to hear defended cases, the need for drugs to be analysed, and police requests for time for further enquiries were the most common reasons for pre-trial remands. But whatever the reason for remand, the result was that the women found themselves in prison untried, and once there they had everything to gain by applying for legal help. Even if they intended to plead guilty, a solicitor could help them in putting the mitigating circumstances. Not only did these defendants have every incentive to ask for legal assistance, but in prison they were given every opportunity to do so. Although notices about legal aid are provided in police stations, and information is printed on charge sheets, these printed instructions seemed to make no impact on the women. In Holloway every prisoner on reception was fully informed about legal aid facilities, and over half of the untried women applied for legal help, although few had done so before they came to prison.

For those who were remanded after conviction events turned out very differently. When they appeared in court, their cases were heard forthwith, and they were sent to prison for social and medical enquiries. For them, once this stage was reached, the incentive to apply for legal aid was much less than it was for those who still had to face their trial. The time when legal advice would have helped these women was before they pleaded; had they had it, it is unlikely that three quarters of those who denied any offence would have pleaded guilty. As it was, by the time the con-victed remands reached Holloway they had pleaded, been asked what they had to say, and said it—or failed to. Nevertheless, when they got to prison, these women, like all receptions, were told about legal aid, although they must also have learned that, except for appeals, it was rarely granted to those applying after conviction.

Altogether, including those seeking help privately, 25 per cent of the convicted remands, as against 54 per cent of the untried, made some attempt to get legal assistance before they were sentenced. And just as there was less incentive for the convicted women to apply for legal aid, so there was less incentive for the courts to grant it. The figures were given in Table 9, p. 44.

Thus from a comparison of the convicted and untried remands it would seem that an important prerequisite for being represented is a breathing space before trial, in which the defendant is given the time and opportunity to apply for help.

There is, of course, no need to remand untried defendants in custody to afford them this breathing space—remands on bail and procedure by summons have the same effect, provided the accused is made aware of legal aid facilities. The practical value of giving defendants time and opportunity to take advice before they are asked to plead, emerged in two other figures in the magistrates' cases. One was the high rate of representation among those whom magistrates had bailed before trial: of thirty-two such women, fifteen were represented. The other was the number of women among the represented who had been granted police bail before their court appearance: 30 per cent of the represented had been on police bail, compared with 16 per cent of the un-represented. Pre-trial bail, like pre-trial custody, gives the defendant the opportunity to seek help when it is most needed; and there was no doubt that many prisoners who were not bailed or remanded before trial would have responded in the same way had the same opportunity been given to them.

Court Survey

A survey of women offenders appearing before two central London magistrates' courts was carried out as a separate exercise in 1967 : its main object was to try and see how these two courts—from which came 20 per cent of the Holloway sample—selected those they sent to prison, but a certain amount of information about legal representation was also obtained.

Cases dealt with by summons had to be omitted from the study; they comprise motoring offences and non-indictable charges of a minor kind. Excluding them and excluding also women who were committed to higher courts, 857 cases were disposed of by the courts in three months. This sample reflects the special problems of central London, and is not representative of all women coming before the courts—for example, over a third of the proceedings were for shoplifting and a quarter for drunkenness.

In the 857 cases, 82 per cent (700) of the defendants were un-represented, 5 per cent (forty-five) had legal assistance, while for the remaining 13 per cent information could not be obtained. A comparison of the forty-five represented with the 700 unrepresented women gave in general a similar picture to that found among the women in prison. The represented had more social ties, less often lived alone, and more frequently had their own homes. Among the unrepresented there was an excess of older women, aged fifty and above, who were convicted of drunkenness offences. As in the prison sample, the rate of representation was similar for all types of offence except that drunkenness offenders, among whom Irish women featured prominently, were never represented, while drug offenders had legal help most frequently. The plea was again a major distinguishing factor, 60 per cent of the represented as compared with 6 per cent of the unrepresented pleading not guilty. Nevertheless, only a minority of those pleading not guilty were likely to have been represented : the information unfortunately was incomplete, but of 118 contested cases fifty (42 per cent) were known to be unrepresented, and twenty-seven (22 per cent) to be represented.

As in the prison survey, the biggest difference between the represented and unrepresented women was the fact of a remand before trial: 87 per cent of the former, compared with 10 per cent of the latter had been remanded, usually on bail, before the hearing. Again, as in the prison sample, the remands were not often made for the purpose of enabling the defendant to get legal assistance : but whatever the reason for the adjournment, the subsequent waiting period before trial gave to the defendant time and opportunity to seek help.

Conclusions

Although in the lower courts certain kinds of women were more likely than others to seek legal help (e.g. women with family ties, first offenders etc.) even among these groups it was only a small minority who were represented. The only sizeable group of prisoners of whom the majority applied for legal assistance were those who were remanded before trial, and in both the prison and court samples the most significant difference between the represented and unrepresented women was that the former had much more often been remanded untried. The reasons for this were discussed above, and they suggest that if more prisoners are to be given legal help, then more of them need to be informed about the facilities in a neutral atmosphere, and at an appropriate time, that is, before they have to plead. Written notices or informative leaflets in police stations and courts are not enough: they meant little to most of the prisoners, and least of all to those whose needs were greatest, the isolated women and girls who had neither family nor friends to support or advise them in times of trouble.

(1) *Bail*

Does legal help make the grant of bail more likely? The prison survey, which by its nature included only those who had not been bailed, could only be used to discover how far legal representation helped to secure a prisoner's release once she had been remanded to Holloway.

Only six out of some 460 women who were remanded in custody were released before the date fixed for their return to court. It is unlikely to have been a coincidence that not only were they all represented, but all were privately represented. Legal representation ensures that the defendant gets competent assistance: private representation that she gets it forthwith.

Four of the six women were released after their lawyers had successfully applied for bail to a judge in chambers. They had all been remanded untried, and all were released within two days of coming to prison, only because they were privately represented was it possible for their applications to be heard so quickly, and for their lawyers personally to present the case for bail to the judges. Legal aid does not cover a solicitor's personal appearance before a judge in chambers, so if the defendant is legally aided or unrepresented immediate action cannot be taken. The procedure in such cases is for an application form to be sent to the Official Solicitor, on which the prisoner's reasons for requesting bail are explained; the Official Solicitor presents this form to the judge, after a corresponding one from the police—detailing any objections to bail—has also been obtained. At the time of the present survey, it took over a week for a written application to a judge in chambers to come through, so unless repeated remanding or committal was anticipated, there was little incentive for the prisoners to ask for application forms. Also, the completion of these by unrepresented women often presented difficulties; the women frequently did not know whether or why the police had objected to bail; they found it hard to express themselves in writing, and many

54

just did not appreciate what kind of information would be relevant to a request for bail. The interviewers did not usually see bail applications, but sometimes it came to their notice that women with strong claims to be granted bail had wholly failed to make these clear on their forms. Although the Widgery Committee did not consider legal aid to be necessary for bail applications, there seem to be considerable arguments for making it available to unrepresented defendants in the lower courts, and to those wishing to make personal applications to a judge in chambers.

Applications for bail to a judge in chambers were both more frequent and more frequently successful when coming from those who were privately represented. Of eleven women remanded untried who were privately represented, four made applications, all of them successful; of eighty-four women who had legal aid and were remanded untried, ten made applications, none of which were successful; and of seventy-three unrepresented women remanded untried, only one applied for bail to a judge in chambers, again without success.

Among the women remanded after conviction, only two applied for bail to a judge: neither was represented, and neither succeeded. Few of those remanded for medical enquiries knew that these could be carried out on bail, or that they were entitled to apply for it to a judge in chambers. It would be interesting to know what the success rate might have been, if more of these women had had legal help, especially private help. Many came from stable homes, and were not involved in serious offences, so it is unlikely that the police would often have opposed bail.

Apart from the four women released on application to a judge in chambers, two others who had been remanded in custody unrepresented were freed within a few days when they engaged private solicitors to ask the magistrates for bail before the end of the remand period. One of these was case no. 549, described on page 18 : the girl was released after four days in prison, when the solicitor engaged by her father persuaded the magistrates that the medical examination could be carried out on bail. Many other women were remanded for medical reports which might well have been obtained on bail; they differed from this one only in that they had lacked a representative to take immediate action on their behalf.

(2) *Acquittals*

How far legal help improves the chances of acquittal is a question which this study was not designed to answer, but a certain amount of information about acquittals was obtained, and this is discussed below. In this discussion 'acquittal' means a case in which every charge was dismissed: if a woman was charged with several offences, and was acquitted on some, but not all, her case has not been shown as an acquittal; nor has it been counted as one if she was acquitted on the original charge but convicted on a lesser one.

Court Survey

In the survey outlined on p. 52 14 per cent of the women tried by the lower courts were known to have pleaded not guilty, although in 13 per cent of cases information about the plea could not be obtained. Of those pleading not guilty, 29 per cent were acquitted (thirty-five out of 120 women). This acquittal rate is lower than that of 40 per cent reported by Zander[1] but the pattern of offences was very different in the two surveys. Information about representation was incomplete, but it did not suggest that represented women were more often acquitted than others.

Irrespective of their representation, women who pleaded not guilty from prison were less likely to be acquitted than those who had been allowed bail, or who were not remanded. This was already known to be true in higher court cases,[2] and American studies have pointed to the same feature.[3] Further research is needed to ascertain whether it is caused by the difficulty of contesting a case from prison. The figures from the present survey are shown below:

TABLE 10

Court Survey: 120 Women Pleading Not Guilty Before Magistrates' Courts

Remanded	No.	Acquitted No.	%
In custody throughout	12	—	—
On bail throughout	65	21	32
First custody, then bail	8	3	37
Not remanded	35	11	31
Total	120	35	29

Prison Survey

In the cases tried by magistrates' courts (including those later committed for sentence) 160 women were remanded in custody before trial; forty-six of them (29 per cent) either said they would plead not guilty, or were assumed by the result of the case to have done so. The charges against twenty-one of these forty-six were dismissed or withdrawn—an acquittal rate of 45 per cent. There was no significant difference in the proportions acquitted among the represented and unrepresented.

Among the women tried by the higher courts were sixty-four who were remanded in custody before trial: twenty-seven (42 per cent) pleaded not guilty, and fourteen of them (52 per cent) were

56

acquitted. Again, there was no difference in the proportions of represented and unrepresented women who were acquitted.

The time spent by the acquitted women in prison was of some interest: twenty-three were in custody for fifteen days or less, six were there for periods between fifteen days and five weeks; and another six spent more than five weeks in prison, including two women who were in custody respectively for thirteen and twenty-four weeks before they were acquitted. The longest delays were in cases heard at the Central Criminal Court: one woman tried there (she pleaded not guilty but was convicted) spent twenty-nine weeks in custody before her case came to trial.

Seven women who were remanded untried on drugs charges pleaded not guilty, and four were acquitted. In three of these acquitted cases the drugs, when analysed, were found to be aspirin and other legal substances. This is always a possibility in drug charges, and it is clearly desirable to remand such cases on bail whenever practicable.

One prisoner was acquitted on appeal; she was the nineteen year old mother of a young baby, who had pleaded not guilty, unrepresented, to a larceny charge in the magistrates' court. She was found guilty, and committed to Holloway for sentence. In prison she learned about legal aid and appeal procedure and applied for legal aid, which was granted : her solicitor advised an appeal against conviction, and it was successful. Had she been put on probation, or dealt with in any way which did not involve custody, she would have accepted the conviction.

NOTES

1. Zander, M., 'Unrepresented Defendants in the Criminal Courts'. Criminal Law Review, Dec. 1969, p. 632.
2. Gibson, E., 'Time Spent Awaiting Trial', H.M.S.O., 1960. Table 6.
3. Rankin, A., 'The Effect of Pre-Trial Detention.' N.Y. University Law Review, Vol. 39 no. 4, June 1964.

Higher Courts

The survey showed, as do the Criminal Statistics, that, compared with the magistrates' courts, legal representation in the higher courts is not unsatisfactory. These courts, however, deal with only a very small proportion of criminal proceedings—even when motoring cases are excluded, only 5 per cent of all criminal cases are heard at the higher courts; the majority of men and women who are given custodial sentences, are sentenced by the lower courts,[1] and the present survey showed that for women 80 per cent of prison receptions are magistrates' court cases.

The survey showed that the main area where there was a major unfulfilled need for legal representation in the higher courts was among those committed for sentence: while among the trial cases only 7 per cent of the women were unrepresented, among those committed for sentence (where the incidence of imprisonment was higher) the proportion was 33 per cent. More recent figures show that the position remains unsatisfactory. The 1969 Criminal Statistics (which do not, in the legal aid tables, give separate figures for men and women) showed that 15 per cent of those committed for sentence were unrepresented in the higher courts, compared with 2 per cent of trial cases. Since 65 per cent of those committed for sentence were given custodial sentences, this means that in 1969 over a thousand of the 1,676 persons who were unrepresented after such committal must have been imprisoned or sent to Borstal.

Magistrates' Courts

Of 484 women prisoners dealt with by the lower courts, 335 (69 per cent) were unrepresented. As was seen in Section 6 90 per cent of the unrepresented women had never attempted to get legal help, nor had the courts suggested it.

Is there any evidence that prisoners are more frequently represented now than they were at the time of the survey? Since it was carried out, some of the relevant recommendations of the

Widgery Committee have been implemented, in particular the introduction of the contributions scheme, and the improvement of arrangements for telling prisoners about legal aid.

The Committee received evidence from prison staff that prisoners were often inadequately informed about the available facilities, and were liable to have difficulty in understanding written information on the subject. The Committee therefore recommended (para. 333) that certain officers in each prison should be made responsible for ensuring that no accused person in need of legal help should be prevented by ignorance from applying for it. This recommendation was implemented at the end of 1968. While this should have improved the situation in some prisons,—notably the large local men's establishments—it will not have changed the position in Holloway, a local prison uniquely free from problems of overcrowding, where already in 1967 all prisoners were systematically told about legal aid facilities when they were first received. The benefits of the Widgery 'designated officer' scheme had in effect been enjoyed by Holloway's prisoners long before the scheme was brought into effect; but nevertheless the majority of the women did not apply for legal aid. One of the reasons, as was seen in Section 7, was that, except for the minority remanded before trial, information disseminated in prison comes too late : the time when defendants need personal and verbal explanation of the legal aid system is before the case is heard. The survey showed that leaflets in police stations, notices in courts or on charge sheets and summons forms (all of which have become more common since 1967) are no substitute for this: the women did not absorb the printed information.

The contributory legal aid system introduced by the Criminal Justice Act 1967 came into effect late in 1968. Depending on their means, those receiving legal aid can now be required to contribute towards the cost of their defence, the size of the contribution, if any, being assessed after the case is concluded. Those wishing to apply for legal aid are therefore now warned, in court and in prison, that the application may result in their being required to make a contribution. Since the great majority of women prisoners failed to apply for legal aid when it was free, it seems unlikely that they will be more eager to apply when they are liable to be assessed for contributions.

Only a further survey in Holloway would show the present situation. In the meantime, there is one piece of evidence about the representation of those sentenced to imprisonment which postdates the implementation of the new legal aid provisions, and it is not reassuring. This is Michael Zander's survey of the cases coming before fifteen London magistrates courts in the course of a week in June 1969.[2] The survey included men and women, but the majority of the defendants were male. It showed that of thirty persons given custodial sentences by the magistrates (twenty-four imprisoned, six sent to detention centres) two thirds were unrepresented. Among another forty-four defendants who were given suspended prison sentences—and who were therefore almost certain to be imprisoned if they committed a further offence—the proportion unrepresented was 72 per cent. As Zander says, the situation was 'on any view a disturbing one'.[3]

Zander's study also confirmed another finding of the present survey, that representation varies comparatively little with the offence. In his survey, 74 per cent of cases tried before the magistrates were unrepresented, and while there were some differences in this proportion (as in the present study, the rate among public disorder offenders was below, and that of drug offenders above, average) on the whole there was little variation with the type of offence; even among ten persons charged with thefts valued at over £100, only one was represented. It cannot therefore be held that to-day the unrepresented consist largely of those accused of trivial offences: they consist, in the lower courts, of the great majority of those accused of all offences. This remains the case in spite of the growth in legal aid in recent years, for although real, this has been small in relation to the size of the problem:[4] in 1969 only 15 per cent of indictable cases heard summarily had legal aid, and although the proportion of applications which are refused is decreasing (23 per cent in 1967, 18 per cent in 1969)[5] this can have little effect on the overall numbers receiving legal aid, so long as more than 95 per cent of the defendants in the lower courts do not apply for it.[6]

In 1966 the Home Secretary,[7] in pointing out that the contributory legal aid scheme was as favourable to the Exchequer as it was unfavourable to the defendant, also remarked that the opposite was true of other parts of the Widgery Committee's report. It was the defendant who would benefit from the suggested improvement of the legal advice system, and from the Committee's criteria as to when the interests of justice required legal aid to be granted. These criteria, which were summarized in paragraph 180 of the report, said that in summary proceedings the interests of justice generally required the defendant to be legally represented when

(a) the accused was in real jeopardy of losing his liberty, or suffering serious damage to reputation
(b) the charge raised substantial questions of law
(c) the accused was unable, through mental or physical disability or language problems, to understand the proceedings or conduct his own case

(d) the defence involved tracing witnesses, or expert cross examination

(e) representation was desirable in the interest of someone other than the accused (e.g. cases of sexual offences against children.)

On the second reading of the Criminal Justice Bill, the Home Secretary undertook to commend these criteria to the courts at the same time as he brought the contributions scheme into operation, saying

'The Widgery scheme, both the favourable and the unfavourable parts of it from the point of view of the Exchequer ... should come into operation not piecemeal, but as a whole.'[7]

Unfortunately this undertaking has not been honoured, and so far it is mainly the parts of the report favourable to the Exchequer which have been chosen for implementation. The suggested improvements to the legal advice system have not been introduced, and the Committee's criteria as to when the interests of justice require legal aid to be given have never been commended to the courts by Home Office circular.

These criteria, as the summary shows, are not generous, and they fall far short of what the same Committee recommended for the higher courts; there was no recommendation that defendants (even those coming within the criteria) should be asked whether they wish to apply for legal aid, and the Committee begged some fundamental questions: for example, no attempt was made to consider how, without large scale and expert interviewing, the courts could hope successfully to identify those who lack the mental ability to follow the proceedings. Nor did the Committee consider how to solve the problem of those who need legal assistance but who plead guilty while ignorant of the law. Many women in the present survey who needed legal help—especially with bail applications and pleas in mitigation—would have fallen outside the Widgery criteria. Nevertheless, although the Committee recommended only a minimal degree of legal aid in the lower courts, its criteria have never been 'commended' to these courts by the Home Secretary.

Why is this? The Home Office have given two reasons. One is 'That the economics of all-round implementation would have thrown an intolerable burden on central funds;' the other that 'from the point of view of solicitor and barrister man-power, it was unrealistic to hope to provide the sort of service to legally-aided defendants which the recommendation of the criteria might have involved.'[8] These reasons can only mean that the Home Office has estimated that a very substantial number of defendants who would be entitled to legal aid under the criteria are not receiving it.[9] If, after the Widgery criteria have been publicly accepted by the Home Secretary, it has been decided within the Home Office that they cannot be implemented, then the whole subject should be looked at afresh.

The object of the present study was to see how prisoners fare under the present system of legal aid, and it was beyond its scope either to devise a more satisfactory system, or to assess the cost, in manpower and finance, of providing one. It could certainly not be done on the cheap, although compensating savings would probably be achieved: it seems likely that if their circumstances were made known to the court by an articulate spokesman, some of those now sent to prison on remand or sentence would be dealt with by non-custodial means. This would not only save the cost of maintaining the prisoner in custody, but would in many cases prevent the prisoner's family from becoming a charge on public funds. But whatever the savings, a more satisfactory system of legal representation could only be established with increased expenditure, both of money and manpower. On the evidence of the present study and of the more recent surveys by Zander and Borrie, the interests of justice appear to necessitate such expenditure; the existing situation prompts the question asked by Stevens and Abel Smith 'Can we justify depriving persons of their liberty without providing for their defence?'[10]

The importance of gettting independent advice before the court hearing was the fundamental point which emerged repeatedly in the course of the present survey. It was the failure to get advice in time, and indeed the failure to realize that advice was necessary, that led women to plead guilty to charges they denied. The Howard League, in their evidence to the Widgery Committee, stressed this point, and suggested that in the larger towns a day and night emergency legal service should be available to persons held at police stations. Another proposal put to the Committee was the introduction of 'duty' solicitors into magistrates' courts. Such a system exists in Scotland, where solicitors attend courts daily to give preliminary legal advice to defendants before they are asked to plead. The great advantage of a scheme like this is that it enables defendants, with the minimum of difficulty and in a more or less routine way, to receive advice before they appear in court: cases which need legal help, which raise questions of law, or to which there is a clear defence, can be identified, and the defendant can be advised accordingly.

The Committee rejected both those proposals, and did not recommend that legal advice should generally be available to accused persons before they appeared in court:[11] if legal advice (or aid) was wanted, the Committee saw as a general rule, no alternative to adjourning the case. This recommendation, however, involves disadvantages. The first is that most accused persons are not asked in court whether they want to apply for legal aid, nor did the Widgery Committee suggest they should be asked. Although leaflets and notices explain the scheme, it was found that the defendants in the present study—most of whom appeared in court the day after being arrested—did not absorb this written information; verbal explanation is needed if those who are not invited by the court to apply for legal aid are to understand the scheme sufficiently well to ask for it themselves, before the case is heard. The second difficulty is that it was not unusual for defendants, even where they knew of the existence of the legal aid scheme, to be unaware of their own need for legal advice, particularly where they did not appreciate the legal implications of the charge, or where they had become persuaded that it was in their interests to plead guilty although they denied the offence. Thirdly, as seen in Section 4, one of the reasons women pleaded guilty to charges they denied was their wish to 'get it over' and their fear of being remanded, especially in custody.[12]

The Widgery Committee rejected the idea of introducing 'duty' solicitors into English courts on the ground that 'it would be almost impossible to make arrangements for (them) to attend the sittings of approximately a thousand courts' ... (paragraph 207). While there would certainly be problems in introducing duty solicitors into every single court, such a scheme could perhaps be tried on an experimental basis, in the busier courts : it has been shown that 36 per cent of all indictable offences take place in seven cities,[13] and courts in these might be suitable starting places for such experiments.

Substantial expansion and reorganization of the legal aid and advice system would be necessary if more defendants are to receive legal advice before pleading. The present study showed how those in prison can be seriously handicapped by the lack both of legal advice, and of a spokesman to defend their interest. The Lord Chief Justice[14] has said, of prisoners facing trial in the higher courts, 'There are of course times when a prisoner can conduct his own defence or make a plea in mitigation more effectively in person and without legal representation. But such a case is of course rare. . . .' The evidence of the survey was that these words are as true of prisoners before the magistrates' courts as they are of high court defendants.

Two final points about the implications of the survey should be made. One is that although it was only concerned with prisoners, its findings do not apply to prisoners alone; if a prison sample shows, for example, that mentally ill persons and those without

63

a knowledge of English are tried unrepresented, then the same is also happening among the far larger number of defendants who do not reach prison. Secondly, perhaps a word should be said about the fact that this study applied only to women. Women after all play only a minor part in the criminal scene, and their role in the criminal legal aid budget must be correspondingly unimportant. Whether women are more or less likely to seek legal help than men is not known, but Zander's study of 1969, referred to above, showed that in trials at magistrates' courts, where the defendants were predominantly male, 74 per cent of all those tried, and two thirds of those given custodial sentences, were unrepresented. This does not suggest that the low rate of representation in Holloway is to be attributed to the sex of the prisoners. Nor is there any reason to believe that the kinds of problems revealed by the survey do not also occur among men—although in some areas, especially that of inconsistent pleading, it would be very interesting to know if they occur on the same scale.

NOTES

1. In 1967, 64% of those sentenced to imprisonment were sentenced by the lower courts. The proportion has been dropping since then, owing to the effects of the Criminal Justice Act 1967 and in 1969 it was 53% (Criminal Statistics, Tables Ia and IIa)

2. Criminal Law Review, Dec. 1969, p. 632. 'Unrepresented Defendants in the Criminal Courts'.

3. A similar conclusion, in respect of the situation in the West Midlands, was reached by Borrie, Prof. G. J. and Varcoe, J. R. in their report, 'Legal Aid in Criminal Proceedings: a Regional Survey' (paras. 243 and 248).

4. Between 1965 and 1969 the proportion of cases dealt with summarily in which legal aid was granted rose from 1% to 3%.

5. Borrie, Prof. G. J., and Varcoe, J. R., show in their report that this overall decrease masks very varied trends in different courts: in two of the four court areas they studied, the refusal rates were higher in 1969 than in 1967 (para. 109).

6. Criminal Statistics 1969, Table I (a) and XVII.

7. Hansard, Vol. 738, Col. 74.

8. Written comments made in August 1970 on an earlier draft of this paper; permission to quote them here has been granted. These comments show that the Home Office believes the criteria to be unrealistic, and knows that they are not generally applied, Nevertheless when asked in Parliament on Dec. 4th 1970 whether the Widgery criteria were being applied, and whether the Home Office would give guidance to magistrates on them, the Under-Secretary of State replied: 'We have no reason to be aware of any substantial body of disagreement with the criteria, nor do we have any substantial reason to believe they are not fully known to the different courts.' Hansard Col. 1740.

9. The Widgery Committee itself did not take this view: they believed the criteria to be in general use, except in a minority of courts, and because they held that their recommendations would involve no change in the existing general practice, the Committee did not think it appropriate to estimate the cost of implementing the criteria (para. 181).

10. 'In Search of Justice', Brian Abel Smith and Robert Stevens, 1968, Allen Lane.

11. Although the Committee did not consider that the legal advice scheme should give defendants a general right to summon solicitors to a police station, they recommended that the scheme should cover such visits (in working hours) in cases of 'some seriousness,' (para. 221.) This recommendation, and others for the improvement of the legal advice service, have not yet been implemented.

12. In cases sent for trial at the higher courts, these difficulties do not exist, for all defendants are subjected to a pre-trial waiting period before they plead, in the course of which they are normally asked whether they wish to apply for legal help.

13. Crime in England and Wales, McClintock, F. H. and Avison, N. Howard, Heinemann, London, 1968.

14. Parker, L. C. J., quoted in an appendix to Home Office circular 90/1961.